"Many people in the U.S. (up to 15%–20% of the U.S. population, according to a Forbes newsletter) and around the world are identified as neurodivergent. As discussions around neurodivergence and neurodiversity have become more common over the past few years, companies are looking for ways of neurodivergent workers to better contribute their talents, skills, and perspectives to directly benefit organization's mission and help improve productivity and performance. This book should be a must-read for readers and organizations interested in recruiting, hiring, retaining, and advancing neurodivergent workers to achieve a competitive edge and bring financial and cultural benefits."

— **Sohel M. Imroz**, *Ph.D., SHRM-SCP, Associate Professor of Human Resource Management, David B. O'Maley College of Business, Florida, U.S.A.*

"This book masterfully explains the importance and steps to improve an organization's talent management processes to set the organization up for success in the changing talent demographics. It is a great reminder to focus on the skills required for a particular position and challenge our bias on unimportant traits. A firm handshake and eye contact never successfully completed a calculus problem."

— **Phillip L. Ealy**, *Ph.D., Penn State University, Pennsylvania, U.S.A.*

"My commendations to Dr. Bill Rothwell and Jonathan Zion for writing about a topic that is long overdue in workforce development! For a long time, small nonprofit organizations have taken on this work to fully integrate neurodiverse people into everyday life. Since the COVID-19 pandemic, the amplification of the talent shortages and attitudes about work have permeated the literature. In contrast, there is a dearth in the literature on ameliorating this crisis. This book shines a light on a viable talent pool and in typical Rothwell fashion, it brilliantly provides practical guides and tips for the HR professional and organizations in adopting broader inclusive practices. I highly recommend adopting this book when preparing young professionals in HR Management, Workforce Development, and Talent Development degree programs as well as professionals in the field."

— **Dr. Cecilia Maldonado**, *Associate Professor, Workforce Development, University of Nevada, Las Vegas*

"In today's world, people and talent remain one of the few sources of sustainable competitive advantage. As the war for talent rages, Rothwell and Zion provide a compelling and unique strategy to winning in the marketplace through the untapped potential of neurodiverse talent. A must-read yet differentiated perspective for anyone looking to boost their organization's talent quotient."

— **Rani Salman**, *Managing Partner, Caliber Consulting*

Winning the Talent War through Neurodivergence

Recruiting talent from among the disabled population poses unique challenges, which often are not adequately addressed by potential employers. Although job seekers presently enjoy an advantage due to global talent shortages, that situation may not continue. Right now, employers are hard pressed to find anyone to fill positions. At this writing, there are two job openings available for every one job applicant to fill it. In that environment, it makes sense for employers to explore alternative ways to get work done and alternative labor groups to do that work. In *Winning the Talent War through Neurodivergence: A Guide for the Neurotypical*, William J. Rothwell and Jonathan D. Zion show how employers can overcome talent shortages by tapping into the often-overlooked pool of talent comprising people with disabilities (PWDs).

Few books examine the human resources processes relating to people with disabilities, and this one provides a range of new insights.

This is a book for anyone involved in developing HR strategies or with responsibility for how human resources are utilized in general, who are interested in improving the methods used to recruit and retain people with disabilities.

William J. Rothwell is Distinguished Professor, Workplace Learning and Performance, at the College of Education, Department of Learning and Performance Systems, The Pennsylvania State University, U.S.A., where he administers a Master's and a Doctoral program in Training and Development/Human Resources.

Jonathan D. Zion has extensive experience engaging with many stakeholders on a variety of disability issues in the workplace and in post-secondary institutions. These stakeholders include social service agencies as well as different levels of management. He holds a Master of Adult Education (M.Ed.) from the Ontario Institute for Studies in Education at the University of Toronto. He lives in Toronto.

Winning the Talent War through Neurodivergence
A Guide for the Neurotypical

William J. Rothwell || Jonathan D. Zion

LONDON AND NEW YORK

First published 2025
by Routledge
2 Park Square, Milton Park, Abingdon, Oxon OX14 4RN

and by Routledge
711 Third Avenue, New York, NY 10017

Routledge is an imprint of the Taylor & Francis Group, an informa business

© 2025 William J. Rothwell and Jonathan D. Zion

The right of William J. Rothwell and Jonathan D. Zion to be identified as authors
of this work has been asserted by them in accordance with sections 77 and 78 of
the Copyright, Designs and Patents Act 1988.

All rights reserved. The purchase of this copyright material confers the right on the
purchasing institution to photocopy pages which bear the photocopy icon and copyright
line at the bottom of the page. No other parts of this book may be reprinted or reproduced
or utilised in any form or by any electronic, mechanical, or other means, now known or
hereafter invented, including photocopying and recording, or in any information storage or
retrieval system, without permission in writing from the publishers.

Trademark notice: Product or corporate names may be trademarks or registered trademarks
and are used only for identification and explanation without intent to infringe.

British Library Cataloguing-in-Publication Data
A catalogue record for this book is available from the British Library

ISBN: 978-0-815-38287-4 (hbk)
ISBN: 978-1-351-20747-8 (ebk)

DOI: 10.4324/9781351207478

Typeset in Times New Roman
by Newgen Publishing UK

William J. Rothwell dedicates this book to his wife, Marcelina V. Rothwell. She is the wind beneath his wings.

Jonathan D. Zion dedicates this book to his family for their years of love and support. To his late parents, David and Irene Zion of blessed memory; to his sister and brother-in-law, Liora and Ariel; and to his nephews, Joel and Joshua.

Contents

Preface	*xi*
Acknowledgments	*xvii*
About the authors	*xviii*
Frequently asked questions (FAQs) about the neurodiverse	*xx*
Advance organizer	*xxv*

1 Talent management and human resources for neurodiversity	1
2 Job requirements and job analysis for neurodiversity	9
3 Job descriptions and job design for neurodiversity	22
4 Recruiting for neurodiversity	38
5 Career management for neurodiversity	50
6 Employee selection for neurodiversity	61
7 Onboarding for neurodiversity	72
8 Training and development for neurodiversity	86
9 Performance management for neurodiversity	98
10 HR trends of the future from a neurodiversity perspective	110

Bibliography	*116*
Index	*119*

Preface

A few years ago, Jonathan D. Zion attended an event intended to bring together students with disabilities and potential employers. There were over a hundred students at various stages of their studies in a variety of post-secondary institutions. Representatives from several large organizations also attended the event. As he listened to the speakers and participated in the workshops, he learned of the tremendous frustration felt by many of the student attendees. One person sitting next to him cried out, "I just want to get a job."

After the program, all the attendees networked with representatives from several large institutions who were present that day. As Jonathan went from the booth of one organization to the next, two things became clear. First, many people representing their organizations had no real desire to be at this event. Their demeanor made it clear that they were there because someone more senior in the organization had instructed them to be there. They did not see the value. Second, they did not have the attitudes and skills to tap into the neurodiverse population. "Go check out opportunities on the website" is not an adequate sentiment when trying to work with potential employees who have special needs. The idea for this book was born on that day. As Jonathan moved between the students and the organizational representatives he experienced a tragic reality. The neurodiverse students and the representatives were in the same room but were worlds apart. It was evident that, if the status quo continued, many students could never realize their unique potential, and many organizations that had set up their booths that day could never tap into the rich talents many neurodiverse students had to offer. That day he remembered thinking to himself, "These people are so close and yet so far apart. How can I bridge the gap between these worlds?"

What qualifies us to bridge the gap?

There was a long road from the conclusions Jonathan came to at the event he described above to this book coming to fruition. The book you are holding in your hands results from ten years of mentoring that started when he came upon one of William J. Rothwell's books while he was in graduate school. Rothwell has 45 years of HR experience, a Ph.D., an MBA, 25 years of teaching experience

xii *Preface*

at Penn State University, and 25 years of experience consulting to organizations around the world. The detailed version of his biosketch can be found at the back of this book.

By the time Jonathan attended that college event, he had 25 years of experience of consciously living with a learning disability (LD) and dealing with its manifestations in multiple settings, including post-secondary institutions and workplaces (including the consulting and education industry) in a major North American city. However, being consciously aware of his disability is one thing. Deciding to share his experience by disclosing the existence of his learning disability to the world was something else. His decision to do so was not an easy one and took much soul-searching. On the one hand, he reached a point where he knew he had valuable insights to share with people trying to tap into the neurodiverse population. His disclosure about himself should make this book more authentic, should give him more credibility with readers, and should help to bring about many of the changes he has hoped for.

He grappled with the ramifications of his disclosure about his disability. What would people think? Would people still accept him for who he is now that they know about his LD? Would anyone listen to what he has to say, and would this disclosure make a difference anyway? Will his being public about his LD have been worth it after all? Those were just some of the questions he wrestled with as he pondered whether to disclose his LD for the sake of writing this book.

He appreciates that everyone has something unique, a talent, to contribute to the world. For some people, those contributions are easy to spot. Some people are naturally gifted athletes, artists, musicians, or scientists. In Jonathan's case, his unique talent was not so apparent. After much introspection, he realized that he, too, had been given a unique gift. On the one hand, he has an LD. He didn't ask for it. That's the way he was born. That disability has allowed him to experience the world in a way he would never have seen and experienced had he not had a disability. He can also express himself in oral and written language. He needed to have both to share the insights he contributed to this book. Without the disability, he would not have the unique experiences he has had in his life. Many people with disabilities are unable to express themselves in the manner that Jonathan can. With Jonathan's unique attributes, he can act as a bridge between the neurodiverse world and the neurotypical world. The experience he had at that event made such a profound impression on him he felt compelled to discuss it with his mentor William J. (Bill) Rothwell.

At first, our conversations centered upon the problem with recruiting from the neurodiverse community, since talent acquisition was the focus of the event he described above. However, after many discussions, we realized that the problem that needed to be solved was not merely one of recruiting from the neurodiverse community. We experienced our flash of insight when we realized that the problem was more global. Sourcing workers is only one piece of the much larger HR puzzle that must be changed to be more attuned to the needs of the neurodiverse community.

Rather than focusing on recruiting, we realized that HR practices needed to change for organizations to successfully benefit from all that neurodiverse employees have to offer. To tackle this question two perspectives would be needed. First, a global perspective on the HR process. Second, the perspective of someone who has seen and experienced the workforce from a neurodiverse perspective. Jonathan had departed from the cocoon and the structure of post-secondary institutions where clear procedures existed to address neurodiversity-related matters. Jonathan spent much time in the workplace and had graduated from the school of hard knocks. We realized that, by bringing together our perspectives, we were uniquely positioned to work on this complex problem. So our respective journeys came together.

We feel confident in saying that what we offer you is unique. It's rare for members of the neurodiverse community to be open about who they are. To the best of our knowledge, no other book revisits HR from a neurodiverse perspective, and to the best of our knowledge there is no other HR book that results from a collaboration between an expert in HR/talent management and someone with a learning disability.

Why will this book be helpful to you?

Unfortunately, the situation Jonathan experienced at the event he described above is just a small piece of a more complex puzzle that is the state of neurodiversity in the workplace today. If you're an employer, you probably find it difficult to fill any position—let alone find first-rate talent. Although the job market now mostly favors employees, this situation will eventually revert to the employers' advantage. Still, there will always be a need to fill positions, and employers should consider as many possible sources of talent as possible to meet future needs. The neurodiverse community represents a largely untapped labor pool for your organization to consider.

Read this book if you want to fare better than the organizations whose representatives attended the event I described above. "Ok, I want to do better than the folks at that event," you say, "but where do I start?" We offer you this book as a companion on your journey to win the talent war through neurodiversity.

Who are the neurodiverse community in this book?

You could be forgiven for feeling overwhelmed at making sense of the notion of disabilities. After all, the neurodiverse population is not homogeneous. In this book when we refer to the neurodiverse community, we refer to people with learning or other non-visible disabilities. We focused on people with learning disabilities and non-visible disabilities for two reasons. First, that is Jonathan's experience. Jonathan has a learning disability, and so that is his frame of reference. He feels best positioned to offer insights based on that experience as opposed to the experience of someone who has another disability, for example. The second reason we focused on learning disabilities and non-visible disabilities is that interventions

xiv *Preface*

to help people with non-visible disabilities reach full productivity can be more complicated and vexing than those required for people with visible disabilities.

Let's be clear: we're not minimizing the challenges faced by people with visible disabilities such as mobility disabilities. However, when dealing with people with visible disabilities, the problems can be more easily defined, as are the solutions (adapted washrooms and workspaces, for example). Therefore, we refer to the neurodiverse community as people with learning disabilities and other non-visible disabilities because we feel that is where we can contribute to the advancement of the neurodiverse community in the workplace.

The Learning Disability Association of Canada (LDAC) in 2002 adopted a definition of learning disabilities that is quoted on their website. To start, one must know what learning disabilities are not: resultant from one's socio-economic status, being visually or hearing impaired, behavioral disorders, or derived from laziness. (These additional factors may, however, only complicate a learning disability.)

In its essence, they maintain that learning disabilities fall into a variety of (what they refer to as) invisible, lifelong disorders – manifested by genetics, injury, or neurobiological factors – affecting one's ability to assimilate, understand, impart, and retrieve verbal or nonverbal information, and can range in severity.

While those who have learning disabilities are typically of average intelligence or higher, they suffer from an impairment in processing or perceiving information, recollecting, or learning.

This can include, but is not limited to, decision-making, oral comprehension, visual comprehension, problem-solving or mathematics, long-term planning, visual-spatial processing, and attention spans.

On a social level, those with learning disabilities may very well have challenges with interaction with others, seeing things from another point of view, understanding how they're being perceived, and organizational skills.

It is critical that a learning disability is recognized and assessed to facilitate skill instructions, coping mechanisms, means of accommodation, and any other adjustments necessary. Doing so will prevent any difficulties or challenges at home, work, school, or in other social interactions.[1]

Why we wrote this book

Finally, a note on why we wrote this book. By writing this book, we wish to inspire a movement of people committed to the success of people with neurologically based disabilities in the workplace. We envision a world where people from the neurodiverse community can thrive at work. We look forward to a world where neurodiverse employees are sought after as employees of choice and valued for the unique talents they possess and for the valuable contributions they can make to organizations regardless of size, sector, or industry. Just as the Berlin Wall kept people from the east moving to the west, too many of the prevailing attitudinal barriers act as Berlin-type walls that either keep people from the neurodiverse community out of organizations altogether or sideline them when they get there. With this book, we invite you to join a community of people around the world chipping away at those walls one brick at a time.

We also hope this book will serve as a catalyst for the crucial conversations within organizations and between organizations needed to transform workplaces. Are we ready to authentically integrate neurodiverse employees in our organizations? Do we know how to listen? Do we care? Are we willing to provide the mandated accommodations seamlessly? Are we willing to treat our neurodiverse colleagues as people worthy of meaningful careers, or are we content to leave them in the shadows of our society or our organizations? We urge you to address these and related questions throughout your organizations and at all levels of the organization chart so that neurodiverse employees can thrive and so your organizations can benefit from all that they have to offer.

Regardless of where you fit on the organization chart, how long you've been in your organization, and what sector or industry you're in, you can make a difference to your organization's ability to become more sensitive to the neurodiverse community. You can listen; you can be authentic; you can be sincere; you can be intentional; and, you can bring down many of the attitudinal barriers that stand in the way of acceptance in organizations today. We hope that with the crumbling of those attitudinal barriers, neurodiverse employees around the world can hold their heads high and be proud of their contributions.

Here's wishing you much success.

How is this book organized?

The Preface explains what prompted the authors to write this book. The Advance Organizer helps readers zero in on issues so that it is possible to identify only those chapters of primary interest to those readers.

Chapter 1 is entitled **Talent Management and Human Resources for Neurodiversity** and makes a case for focusing on neurodiverse populations as a way to win the talent war. It defines key terms and lists issues for employers, and HR practitioners, to consider. **Chapter 2** is entitled **Job Requirements and Job Analysis for Neurodiversity**, and it explains – in a fictional frame of an employer facing a challenge followed throughout the book – of how to conceptualize work in the context of neurodiverse workers. **Chapter 3** builds on Chapter 2 and describes how to rethink job descriptions and job design for neurodiverse workers. **Chapter 4** is about recruitment, reinvented so that employers are better positioned to attract neurodiverse workers. **Chapter 5** describes career management for neurodiverse workers, providing a "what's in it for me" for workers to care about their future. **Chapter 6** is about employee selection, describing how picking the right workers can be done in ways that will be sensitive to the neurodiverse. **Chapter 7** is about onboarding, a critical step in talent management because first impressions of an employer count with employees and because early socialization matters to help retain talented workers. **Chapter 8** is about training and developing neurodiverse people. **Chapter 9** is about performance management, focused on the needs of

xvi *Preface*

neurodiverse workers. Finally, **Chapter 10** concludes the book, making predictions about HR and relating those to the needs of neurodiverse workers.

We are your partners on your journey to winning the talent war through neurodivergence.

William J. Rothwell
State College, Pennsylvania

Jonathan D. Zion
Toronto, Ontario
January 2025

Note

1 www.ldac-acta.ca/learn-more/ld-defined/ (Accessed on 01/26/2018); www.ldac-acta.ca/learn-more/ld-defined/a-working-description-of-learning-disabilities/ (Accessed on 01/26/2018)

Acknowledgments

I am grateful to my late parents, David and Irene Zion, of blessed memory, for a life time of love, warmth and support.

Thank you for a lifetime of love, warmth, and support.

In his work and beyond, my father applied his financial skills for the benefit of his community. My mother, as an educator, was deeply committed to helping all of her students develop their potential to the fullest, particularly those from disadvantaged backgrounds who faced many challenges.

I continue to be inspired by them, and with this book I hope to follow the examples my parents set of using their talents for the benefit of others who are in need. I have written this book in the sincere hope of making a positive contribution to the world of work and the neurodiverse community by helping to create workplaces where people with neurologically based disabilities may thrive.

I greatly appreciate the help from the following family members and friends who gave of their time to read the manuscript and share their feedback. Thank you, Dad, Liora, and Ariel. Thank you to Andrea, Penne, Avraham, Tamara and Ariel.

Ari, thank you for being a friend in a million.

Thank you to Matthew Ranscombe, Christiana Mandizha and Kristina Abbotts at Taylor and Francis for all your time, effort, attention to detail, and support in helping to bring this book to fruition.

About the authors

William J. Rothwell, Ph.D., DBA, SPHR, SHRM-SCP, RODC, FLMI, CPTD Fellow, is President of Rothwell & Associates, Inc., Rothwell & Associates, LLC, Rothwell & Associates Korea, and a partner in The Rothwell Partnership.

As a consultant, William J. Rothwell has worked with over fifty multinational companies and countless governments and nonprofits. In addition to the three consulting companies he founded, he also founded three small businesses in State College, PA (a vacation rental home company employing three people; a personal care home for the elderly licensed for fifty beds employing twenty-seven people; and an eighteen-unit motel employing nine people). Before joining Penn State in 1993, he had nearly 20 years of executive-level work experience in human resources, talent development, and Organization Development leadership in government (the Illinois Office of the Auditor General) and in business (Franklin Life Insurance Co., a wholly-owned subsidiary of American Brands, a multinational company, #48 on the Fortune 500 list). With a combined total of fifty years of work experience in HR, OD, and Talent Development, he has published 170 books in the Human Resources and related fields and has delivered over 1,600 professional presentations in 15 nations over a 30 year period.

As a Distinguished Professor at Penn State University, University Park, where he has taught for 31 years, he is a leader of an online and onsite academic program that offers a master's degree in Organization Development and Talent Development (see www.worldcampus.psu.edu/degrees-and-certificates/penn-state-online-organization-development-and-change-masters-degree) and chairs doctoral committees in Workforce Education and Development with an emphasis in Talent Development/Organization Development (see https://ed.psu.edu/workforce-education-and-development-doctoral-degree).

Recent Publications

His recent books since 2020 include *Motivated to Stay* (2025), *Revolutionizing the Online Learning Journey: 1,500 Ways to Increase Engagement* (2024), *Beyond Diversity, Equity, and Inclusion: Creating a Culture of Enduring Social Impact* (2024), *The Inclusive, Empathetic, and Relational Supervisor* (2024), *Accelerated*

Action Learning (2024), *Building an Organizational Coaching Culture* (2024), *Mastering the Art of Process Consultation and Virtual Group Coaching Simulation* (2023); *Successful Supervisory Leadership* (2023); *Effective Succession Planning*, 5th ed (2023); *Transformational Coaching* (2023); *Succession Planning for Small and Family Businesses* (2022); *High-Performance Coaching for Managers* (2022); *Rethinking Diversity, Equity, and Inclusion* (2022); *Organization Development (OD) Interventions: Executing Effective Organizational Change* (2021); *Virtual Coaching to Improve Group Relationships* (2021); *The Essential HR Guide for Small Business and Start Ups* (2020); *Increasing Learning and Development's Impact Through Accreditation* (2020); *Adult Learning Basics*, 2nd ed. (2020); and, *Workforce Development: Guidelines for Community College Professionals*, 2nd ed. (2020).

Jonathan D. Zion has extensive experience engaging with many stakeholders on a variety of disability issues in the workplace and in post-secondary institutions. These stakeholders include social service agencies as well as different levels of management. He holds a Master of Adult Education (M.Ed.) from the Ontario Institute for Studies in Education at the University of Toronto. He lives in Toronto. He can be reached by email at jonathanzion@rogers.com.

Frequently asked questions (FAQs) about the neurodiverse

When managers and HR professionals first think about issues associated with neurodiversity, they may have many predictable questions. The questions and answers below are an effort to address some of them.

Question 1: Why do you prefer the word "neurodiverse" instead of simply calling people "disabled"?

Language matters. Some people find the word "disabled" to be as offensive, as they do the word "handicapped." We do not mean to be insensitive when we use the word "disabled" for people with disabilities. Since many *invisible* disabilities are caused by neurological conditions, the word "neurodiverse" seems appropriate. It is important to distinguish neurologically rooted conditions from *visible* physical disabilities.

Question 2: Why should anyone care about the neurodiverse community? How does that relate to business needs?

Baby Boomers are retiring around the world, and some nations face a shortage of qualified workers to fill job vacancies. Employers should explore alternative labor sources to meet labor demands. The neurodiverse community comprises one such group.

Question 3: Why do HR professionals need to know about the neurodiverse community?

There is a tendency by managers and by HR professionals to make quick judgments about job applicants. One research study found, for instance, that interviewers decide within the first six minutes of an interview if a job applicant is acceptable (Zolfagharifard, 2014). Neurodiverse employees are at a disadvantage when superficial impressions such as eye contact or handshakes govern employment actions because they may (depending on the condition which applicants may experience) look or behave differently from neurotypical workers. HR professionals need to be made more aware of these issues and sensitized to them if they are to choose productive, qualified workers.

Question 4: How does a manager or HR professional know that an employee experiences a neurological condition?

There are three ways.

First, the employee knows about his or her neurological condition and willingly describes it to the manager or HR professional. At that point, the manager or HR professional may ask for evidence to support that assertion, such as a doctor's diagnosis. If the employee does not have that diagnosis, the manager or HR professional may direct the worker to secure that diagnosis if it can be obtained – and not all can be proven.

Second, the employee knows about his or her neurological condition but conceals it, out of fear of the consequences, from the manager or HR professional. In this situation, the manager or HR professional must recognize the condition by getting to the reasons why the employee cannot achieve necessary work results or demonstrates behaviors considered unusual by co-workers. The manager or HR professional may direct the individual to the Employee Assistance Program but does not reduce or make any effort to achieve reasonable accommodation until a diagnosis is secured. In any case, the employee and the manager should work together to determine appropriate ways for the worker to demonstrate the job performance the organization requires.

Third, neither employee nor manager/HR professional knows that the neurological condition exists. It is necessary to diagnose it and then work with it. That requires performance analysis.

Question 5: What is performance analysis?

Performance analysis is the systematic process of diagnosing why workers do not perform their jobs. The topic is too big to address here. But many books have examined it. See for instance:

- Fournies, F. (2007). *Why employees don't do what they're supposed to do and what to do about it*. 2nd ed. New York: McGraw-Hill Education.
- Mager, R., & Pipe, P. (1997). *Analyzing performance problems*. 3rd ed. Atlanta, GA: Center for Effective Performance.
- Robinson, D., Robinson, J., Phillips, J., Phillips, P. & Handshaw, R. (2015). *Performance consulting: A strategic process to improve, measure, and sustain organizational results*. 3rd ed. San Francisco: Berrett-Koehler.
- Rothwell, W. (2015). *Beyond training and development: Enhancing human performance through a measurable focus on business impact*. 3rd ed. Amherst, MA: HRD Press.
- Rothwell, W. et al. (2013). *Performance consulting: Applying performance improvement in human resource development*. San Francisco: Pfeiffer.
- VanTiem, D., Moseley, J. & Dessinger, J. (2012). *Fundamentals of performance improvement: Optimizing results through people, process, and organizations*. 3rd Edition. San Francisco: Pfeiffer.

xxii *Frequently asked questions (FAQs) about the neurodiverse*

Question 6: How do managers or HR professionals deal with individuals who have job performance problems but do not have neurological conditions?
Managers and HR professionals should apply the principles of performance consulting. The books cited in response to Question 2 provide clues to answer this question. There are many reasons why people do not perform their jobs, and each cause may require one or more different solutions.

Question 7: How does a manager or HR professional explain to other workers why neurodiverse employees receive different treatment?
That is a tough question. In some nations, such as the U.S.A., managers should avoid discussing worker issues with other workers due to employee privacy laws, rules, and court rulings. It may be necessary to indicate to workers that the actions management is taking to get appropriate results are essential. Further elaboration may not be appropriate. Managers can cite employee privacy laws as the reasons why they cannot elaborate on their reasons for taking the actions they take. If workers are persistent in asking why one worker is treated differently from others, managers may need to seek advice on how to field such questions from the HR department or the legal department.

Question 8: How does a manager or HR professional deal with workers who pretend that they experience neurological conditions but do not have them?
There is a risk that, if some workers are treated differently from others, workers will find out why and will try to seek the same reasonable accommodations even though some workers do not need them. There is no shortcut for managers, or HR professionals, to conduct their due diligence investigation to reach their diagnosis of causes for performance problems.

Question 9: How do managers or HR professionals surface neurological conditions during the selection process?
Neurodiverse workers are often fearful that, if they reveal their conditions during job interviews or on application forms, they will not be chosen for jobs. Hence, there may be a proclivity to conceal that information.

If employers have cultivated a reputation – that is, developed an employment brand – for sensitivity to the needs of disabled workers, then job applicants will be more likely to reveal their conditions. The opposite is also true: if employers have a reputation for not being sensitive to the needs of the disabled, then workers will be more likely to conceal the information during the selection process.

It is helpful to use performance tests during the selection process to see if workers have the ability to learn or perform the work. For instance, an individual applying for an executive assistant job might be asked to edit a document using Word. Similarly, professionals may be given work simulations in which they are asked to demonstrate the ability to perform the work.

Question 10: Corporate culture is key to creating a work environment that values people with neurologically based disabilities. How does an organization

Frequently asked questions (FAQs) about the neurodiverse xxiii

establish a corporate culture within which the end-to-end talent management process can be re-examined? What competencies do organizational leaders need to have to foster such a culture?

Managers often say they wish to "change the corporate culture." But the reality is that corporate culture is a result of the collective experience and history of an organization. As a consequence, the only way to change corporate culture is to give the organization new experiences. If those experiences are successful, people learn to behave that way; if they are unsuccessful, people learn to avoid behaving that way.

Changing the corporate culture is a long-term effort. It requires leadership from the top and many other actions. The field of Organization Development is about changing corporate culture. It is a topic too big to cover here. But readers who are interested in corporate culture change are well-advised to read the how-to information appearing in such books as these:

- Rothwell, W. (Ed.). (2015). *Organization development fundamentals: Managing strategic change*. Alexandria, VA: ATD Press.
- Rothwell, W., Stavros, J., & Sullivan, R. (Eds.). (2015). *Practicing organization development: Leading transformation and change*, 4th ed. New York: Wiley.

Question 11: What organizations are considered best-practice firms in addressing the needs of neurodiverse employees?

No list exists of so-called "best-practice firms" in dealing with neurodiverse employees.

But one article lists such organizations as Microsoft and SAP as working with autistic employees (Felicetti, n.d.). They are addressed individually, and there are hundreds of neurodiverse conditions. Each one must be separately examined for organizations that support or employ people with those conditions.

Question 12: How do such measures of business results as productivity, profitability, safety, and others relate to changing the talent management process to meet the needs of neurodiverse employees?

Each neurodiverse condition must be examined separately, just as individual workers must be examined for their unique needs. Not all individuals are the same. But the reality is that neurodiverse workers do not comply with the stereotype of being unproductive.

Consider that while more than 10 percent of Americans battle at least one form of disability (Cornell Chronicle, 2013), they (and their families) collectively earn more than a quarter of a trillion dollars each year. Statistics, moreover, reveal a telling fact: those who had experience managing workers with disabilities are "overwhelmingly likely" to recommend the hiring of workers with disabilities. (Those very managers might also be able to acknowledge that meeting federal standards for accommodating those with disabilities can cost a negligible amount or nothing at all (Cornell Chronicle, 2013)).

xxiv *Frequently asked questions (FAQs) about the neurodiverse*

While these statistics are weighted toward those with physical disabilities, it is clear that people with mental or neurological problems face major challenges in employment (Stuart, 2006). That includes people who have what is called *Attention Deficit Trait* (Hallowell, 2005).

Question 13: Do some employers worry that neurodiverse employees expect special treatment, what some call an "entitlement mentality"?

Individuals differ. While some neurodiverse workers may expect special treatment, employers are obligated to make reasonable accommodations only. We are not saying that business needs should be sacrificed on the altar of political correctness.

Question 14: What obligations do neurodiverse workers have to their employers?

Neurodiverse workers, once hired, may be reluctant to discuss known conditions with their employers. They may fear what can happen when and if they do so. That fear is understandable. In some organizations, it is a genuine concern because there may be consequences, real or imagined, that stem from revealing the condition.

But neurodiverse workers do owe it to their employers to get the results that their jobs demand. They should take steps necessary to achieve that goal.

Advance organizer

Complete the following Organizer before you read the book. Use it as a diagnostic tool to help you assess what you most want to know about making the most of a prospective new sources of talent – the neurodiverse – and where you can find information about ways to reinvent human resources to tap that source of traditionally overlooked talent.

The organizer

Directions

Read each item in the Organizer below. Circle a *True (T)*, a *Not Applicable (N/A)*, or *False (F)* in the left column opposite each item. Spend about ten minutes on the Organizer. Be honest! Think of HR as you would like it to be – not what some expert says it is or what you think your organization is presently doing. When you finish, score and interpret the results using the instructions appearing at the end of the Organizer. Then be prepared to share your responses with others you know to help you think about what you most want to learn about demonstrating sensitivity to neurodiverse people. If you would like to learn more about one item below, refer to the number in the right column to find the chapter in this book in which the subject is discussed.

The questions

HR practitioners should

Circle your response for each item below: *Chapter in the book in which the topic is covered*:

xxvi *Advance organizer*

Does your organization

T N/A F	1. Describe Human Resources in a way that is attuned to needs of neurodiverse people?	1
T N/A F	2. Identify job requirements and conduct job analysis in ways aligned with needs of neurodiverse people?	2
T N/A F	3. Write job descriptions and design jobs in ways sensitive to neurodiverse people?	3
T N/A F	4. Carry out recruiting in ways suitable to neurodiverse people?	4
T N/A F	5. Manage career issues in ways appropriate for neurodiverse people?	5
T N/A F	6. Select employees in ways sensitive to the neurodiverse community?	6
T N/A F	7. Carry out onboarding of new hires in ways appropriate for neurodiverse people?	7
T N/A F	8. Train and develop people in ways aligned with the needs of the neurodiverse?	8
T N/A F	9. Carry out performance management efforts in ways sensitive to neurodiverse people?	9
T N/A F	10. Plan for HR based on future trends?	10
____ Total		

Scoring and interpreting the organizer

Give yourself *1 point for each T* and a *0 for each F or N/A* listed above. Total the points from the *T* column and place the sum in the line opposite to the word **TOTAL** above. Then interpret your score as follows:

Score

10–9 points = *Congratulations! Give your organization grade of A.* Your organization is demonstrating sensitivity to the neurodiverse.

8–7 points = *Give your organization a grade of B.* Your organization is making progress in demonstrating sensitivity to the neurodiverse.

6–5 points = *Give your organization a grade of C.* Your organization is about average, and that means your organization should take steps to improve sensitivity to neurodiverse people.

4–3 points = *Give your organization a grade of D.* Your organization is below average. That means you need to play catch up to compete for the talent represented by neurodiverse people.

2–0 points = *Give your organization a failing grade.* Take immediate steps to improve how well your organization addresses issues important to neurodiverse people so as to attract, develop, and retain an important potential source of talent.

1 Talent management and human resources for neurodiversity

The world faces a talent crisis. Too few children are being born, many people are living longer due to improved healthcare, and too few well-qualified people are available to fill job vacancies in some booming economies. To fill future positions when too few young people can be recruited, employers should look to labor groups that are traditionally underrepresented. One such group is the *neurodiverse community*, defined as people who have so-called "invisible disabilities" such as learning disabilities, autism, schizophrenia, obsessive-compulsive disorder (OCD), dyslexia (we've used the word dyslexia because many laypeople still use it even though experts currently refer to this as a learning disability in reading), and so many others that are primarily neurologically based. They are "invisible" because, unlike visible disabilities such as loss of a limb, employers cannot see them.

This chapter scopes the global challenge. First, the chapter dramatizes the issues through a series of compelling scenarios. Second, it describes demographic matters globally. Third, it examines global labor demand. Fourth, it reviews alternative approaches to meeting labor needs. Fifth and finally, the chapter looks at how and why Human Resources Management (HRM) should be redefined to tap traditionally underserved labor groups – and specifically how HR can better address issues associated with the neurodiverse community as a means to win the talent war.

The challenge

How is your organization handling talent management and human resource issues at a time of talent shortages? Read the following vignettes and, on a separate sheet, describe how *your* organization would solve the problem presented in each. If you can offer a practical solution to all the challenges described in the vignettes, then your organization may already have effective ways to address workforce challenges in place; if not, your organization may have an urgent need to devote more attention to these issues.

DOI: 10.4324/9781351207478-1

2   Talent management and human resources for neurodiversity

Vignette 1

A job applicant walks into an HR office. During the job interview, the applicant does not look the interviewer in the eye. Afterward, the HR representative discounts the excellent resume that matches the work requirements because the applicant "seemed evasive in the interview."

Vignette 2

A newly hired executive assistant is a source of stress for her on-the-job trainer. The trainer reports to their supervisor that "the new hire seems to need to re-learn how to use Word each day." She is let go at the end of the first week. Crying after she is told she is fired, the executive assistant admits she has a learning disability.

Vignette 3

A supervisor is upset. She notices that an employee is using an app on his cell phone to record a staff meeting and confronts the employee, asking why he is recording. The employee admits he has a neurological condition that makes it difficult for him to remember things. He apologizes for recording the meeting without permission.

Final remarks

If your organization can address the vignettes described above – and other situations just like them – then your organization is well-positioned to leverage a labor force that has been traditionally overlooked by most employers. But if your organization cannot address the vignettes above, your organization and your HR staff have work to do.

Global demographic issues

Most business people are aware that many nations face demographic challenges.

Consider

- Ten thousand Baby Boomers retire in the U.S. each day (Washington Post, 2014).
- 72.5 million people were born during the Baby Boomer years between 1946 and 1964, and that represents 22.58 percent of the U.S. population of 321 million people in 2015. As they retire, their loss will create significant challenges for the U.S. (Cnn.com, 2017).
- The global healthcare costs associated with an aging population is expected to skyrocket.

- Employers will face difficulties in hiring traditional groups – such as recent college graduates – for the simple reason that there will be fewer people in that group.
- By the mid-2030s, close to 25 percent of Canada's population will be retirement age (Globe and Mail, 2015).
- Declines in population growth are expected in growing economies such as China, India, and Brazil due to falling birth rates, and these declines may affect global economic growth (India Times, 2015).

The point of this section is to emphasize that declining birth rates, combined with increasing longevity, will mean that the world's population is aging (Un.org, 2002). And that poses future challenges for employers in recruiting, onboarding, training, and retaining workers.

Labor demand

It is a great irony of this century that the most populous countries in the world often have too few well-qualified people to fill all the job vacancies that exist in those countries. As long as some parts of the world – particularly those in Asia – lead the world in economic growth, local labor demand in each Asian nation will outstrip supply. And it is sometimes difficult to get accurate figures because government statistics in some countries are notoriously inaccurate (Manzella Report, n.d.). Nor is China alone (Vietnam Briefing, 2014).

Labor shortages are significant because they can provide the basis for population movements across national borders. Labor shortages also lead employers to seek innovative approaches to solving the problems stemming from these shortages.

Alternative approaches to meeting labor needs

When managers and government policymakers think of talent shortages, they tend to be too traditional in their thinking. For instance, when a job vacancy occurs, managers immediately want to recruit from outside or promote from inside. Likewise, when a talent shortage exists on a national level, government policymakers wish to spur immigration (to import talent) or invest in government-sponsored education and training (to develop domestic talent).

Such thinking is too limited. It misses the point that the issue is not to recruit or develop people for jobs but rather to get work done. While that statement sounds simple, the implications are profound because there are many ways to get work done without recruiting or promoting anyone. Automation is one solution. So is job or process simplification. As many as 55 strategies exist to get work done (Rothwell, Graber & McCormick, 2012).

Of course, another idea is to explore tapping underrepresented labor groups. If Baby Boomer retirements are causing problems, then perhaps a solution is to

4 *Talent management and human resources for neurodiversity*

change retirement policies to encourage people to work longer (see Rothwell, Sterns, Spokus & Reaser, 2008). Another idea is to tap historically underrepresented groups such as those with visible (physical) or invisible (neurological) disabilities. This book explores better ways to draw on the untapped talent pool of the neurodiverse community.

What is neurodiversity, and why is neurodiversity important?

A *neurological condition* is related to an individual's central nervous system. Some are genetic; some are acquired. The National Institute of Neurological Conditions and Stroke catalogs over 400 disorders, though other estimates swell the total to more than 600 disorders. Some of the better known include (Brainfacts.org, n.d.):

- Autism
- Autism spectrum disorder
- Dyslexia

> Other 'invisible' conditions that affect individuals have to do with learning disabilities and psychological challenges. Learning disabilities afflict over 4 million children in the U.S. alone and include a broad array of conditions such as communication, developmental articulation, stuttering, reading, writing, and concentration disorders.
>
> (CureResearch.com, 2005)

Psychological conditions, which also constitute invisible disabilities, are identified in *The Diagnostic and Statistical Manual of Mental Disorders* (DSM).

In this book, we categorize people who have neurologically based differences as "the neurodiverse community." These differences may manifest themselves intellectually (such as learning disabilities), socially (such as autism), or emotionally (such as bipolar disorder). It is also possible (and frequently the case) that neurologically based differences may pose intellectual, social, and emotional challenges. This group represents an underutilized human resource that may help meet present and future talent shortages. The group may be vital to winning the so-called talent war.

Consider some facts and figures about the neurodiverse community:

- As of 2007, about a billion people across the globe reportedly struggle with neurological disorders, says a UN study.
- "Up to 10 percent of the population is affected by specific learning disabilities (SLDs), such as dyslexia, dyscalculia, and autism, translating to 2 or 3 pupils in every classroom" (Science Daily, 2013).
- "According to a global study conducted by the World Health Organization, 8 out of 10 disorders in the 3 highest disability classes are neurologic problems" (Speech-Language and Audiology Canada, 2017).

- In 2014 The U.S. National Institute of Mental Health (NIMH) estimated that there were more than 43 million people – or approximately 18 percent of Americans – over age 18 with "any mental illness" within the year (National Institute of Mental Health, 2015).
- Globally, more than 300 million people of all ages suffer from depression (World Health Organization, 2017).
- Autism and autism spectrum disorders are estimated to affect 1 in 68 children living in the U.S., according to a 2012 report from the Centers for Disease Control (Centers for Disease Control and Prevention, 2016).

While progress has been made for physically disabled groups concerning accessibility (though they too remain subject to discrimination), the neurodiverse community is a widely discriminated-against group and consequently experiences high levels of unemployment (Medscape, 2006).

The research notes that those who have "serious mental disorders" are in fact eager to seek, and perform, work, yet suffer from three to five times the level of joblessness than the mainstream population. The statistics say that nearly two-thirds of "working age adults with mental health disabilities" are not gainfully employed, versus a fifth in the non-disabled world.

It is a far-reaching problem for those battling various health issues.

Those facing "serious and persistent psychiatric disabilities" face 80–90 percent unemployment; those with a "major depressive disorder" experience a 40–60 percent unemployment rate; and those with an anxiety disorder, anywhere from 20 to 35 percent.

Suffice it to say, these groups – and others like them – are consequently among the most significant recipients of government assistance and social safety net help.

Exacerbating the situation may very well be the notion that employers could harbor stigmas toward those with mental health challenges.

In fact, statistics reveal that half of the employers concede to being hesitant to hire those with a "psychiatric disability" or a "past psychiatric history or currently undergoing treatment for depression." Nearly 70 percent acknowledged that they might be unwilling to hire someone on prescription antipsychotic medication.

A quarter of employers surveyed indicated they would fire an employee if it was discovered they had not disclosed a mental illness – illegal according to the Americans with Disabilities Act. The Act obligates employers to provide "reasonable workplace accommodations for people with physical and mental disabilities."

Tapping and leveraging the talent of the neurodiverse community may be the next horizon for HR managers and professionals.

Redefining Human Resources Management for neurodiversity

Nobody claims that leveraging the talents of the neurodiverse community will be easy. Government policies must encourage it. And, at the same time, Human

6 *Talent management and human resources for neurodiversity*

Resources Management practitioners must be prepared to make the business case by convincing business leaders that it is worth the time, money, and effort to attract, onboard, develop, retain, and work with the neurodiverse population. Organizations wanting to win the war for talent by tapping into the neurodiverse community need to be willing to re-examine every aspect of the talent management process. Seeds must be planted in fertile soil. So re-examining processes need to take place in the context of an organizational culture that values people with disabilities in general and those with neurologically based differences in particular. They should be regarded as employees of choice and not employees of last resort. Organizational leaders need to have the competencies to foster such a culture.

This chapter scoped the global challenge. First, the chapter dramatized the issues through a series of compelling scenarios. Second, it described demographic matters globally. Third, it examined global labor demand. Fourth, it reviewed alternative approaches to meeting labor needs. Fifth and finally, it examined how and why Human Resources Management (HRM) should be redefined to tap traditionally underserved labor groups – and specifically how HR can better address issues associated with the neurodiverse community as a means to win the talent war.

This book addresses how to redefine HR to support the neurodiverse community. Subsequent chapters describe ways to do that.

A Tool for Reflecting on the Big Picture: How to Adapt HR to the Needs of Neurodiverse Employees

Directions: Use this tool to structure your thinking about how to make HR in your organization attuned to the needs of neurodiverse employees. For each HR issue listed in the left column below, write notes to yourself in the right column about actions to take to make that area more attuned to the needs of people with neurologically based differences. There are no right or wrong answers, though some answers may be better than others. Use this tool to guide a group of people from your organization to consider proposals to make the organization more responsive to the needs of the neurodiverse community.

	HR Issue	How can this HR area be adapted to the needs of the neurodiverse community? Answer with actions to take.
1	Job Requirements and Job Analysis	
2	Job descriptions and Job Design	
3	Recruiting	
4	Career Management	
5	Employee Selection	
6	Onboarding	
7	Training and Development	
8	Performance Management	
9	Corrective Action	
10	Reward Systems	
11	Retaining and Engaging Employees	
12	Promoting Health and Safety	
13	Employee Assistance Programs	

8 *Talent management and human resources for neurodiversity*

What to do after reading this chapter

1 Ask your HR staff to read the vignettes in this chapter.
2 Ask your staff whether they have any experience working or volunteering with disabled people in general and with people with neurologically-based disabilities in particular.
3 Ask some of your recruiting staff how they would feel about attending a recruiting event for people with disabilities. Their first reaction will be very telling.
4 Arrange to have informal meetings with some of your line managers. Ask them how they would feel about an employee or colleague disclosing the existence of a non-visible disability.
5 Have informal meetings with some of your HR staff. Ask them if they are familiar with non-visible disabilities in general and with neurologically based disabilities in particular. Have they heard of these terms? Do they know what they refer to?

2 Job requirements and job analysis for neurodiversity

Job analysis is the foundation of Human Resources Management (HRM). The theory is simple enough, even though the implications are profound. All HR efforts begin with analyzing the work to be performed and then use that information as the basis for recruiting, onboarding, training, developing, appraising, and taking all other HR actions.

If job analysis is essential for neurotypical employees, it is all the more so for neurodiverse employees. Job analysis clarifies what work results are sought from workers and is the foundation for objective efforts to find, develop, and keep people who can achieve those results. Work results can be secured in many ways, and those ways must be considered if the organization is to establish a culture of inclusiveness for neurodiverse workers. It is thus necessary to look beyond "What have we always done to carry out the work?" to "What do we have to do to get work results?" so that employees with neurologically based differences are not ruled out because they cannot do the work in the same ways that other employees have always performed it.

This chapter introduces a fictional case study. The purpose of the fictional frame is to provide the reader with a lens through which to view the end-to-end talent management process from the perspective of an organization that is learning how to adapt its talent management processes to integrate members of the neurodiverse community. First, the chapter uses the fictional frame to reconsider strategic HR planning. Second, the chapter illustrates how several approaches to job analysis should be reconsidered to integrate members of the neurodiverse community into the fictional organization. Third and finally, the chapter demonstrates how job descriptions ought to be reinvented for successfully tapping into the talents of the neurodiverse community.

Strategic HR planning

When you think about how information on jobs is used to examine a company's organizational structure, consider: "What jobs do we need to create, what skills do they require, and are those skills different from those required by the company's current jobs?" (Belcourt, Singh, Bohlander & Snell, 2014).

DOI: 10.4324/9781351207478-2

10 *Job requirements and job analysis for neurodiversity*

Here are questions you should think about as you consider integrating neurodiverse employees into your organization:

- How do we best accommodate neurodiverse employees?
- Do the divisions, departments, or business units where those jobs will be created have cultures to support neurodiverse employees?
- Do we as an organization have the strategic partnerships with social service agencies and providers to ensure that we are positioned to meet the needs of a wide range of neurodiverse employees?

A note on the fictional frame

The underlying premise of this book is that managers and workers in general and HR practitioners, in particular, will need to reflect on how to be different kinds of people if they are to tap into the talents of historically overlooked sources of talent such as the neurodiverse community. For many HR professionals, this means thinking about adopting new attitudes, beliefs, and behaviors relating to people with disabilities in general and the neurodiverse community in particular. This message has the potential to make readers feel threatened and judged. That is not our intention. Like watching a play, it is easier to be in the audience than it is to be on the stage. We decided to use this story-based approach to give readers the opportunity to watch fictional characters wrestle with the issues. With that, let's turn this over to the people at The ABC Company as they start their journey of trying to win their war for talent by integrating the neurodiverse population into their organization.

The next section of this chapter introduces the case study that will be used throughout the book. The topics that will be treated in this chapter include considering strategic HR planning issues, namely, recruitment, selection, training and development, performance appraisal, legal compliance, and job analysis. The chapter illustrates how several common approaches to job analysis, namely, The Position Analysis Questionnaire System, The Critical Incident Method, Task Inventory Analysis, and Competency-Based Analysis, ought to be reconsidered to integrate members of the neurodiverse community into the fictional organization. Finally, this chapter will show how job descriptions ought to be reinvented to be aligned with the goal of drawing on the talents of the neurodiverse community.

Recruitment

Harriet has been an HR manager for The ABC Company, a large organization which employs 50,000 people worldwide, for the last 15 years. She is accustomed to writing job descriptions for the positions she wishes to fill. Conventional thinking has it that a job description states at least the knowledge, skills, and attitudes needed for a worker to perform a job. Job descriptions can be useful tools for attracting qualified candidates (Belcourt, Singh, Bohlander & Snell, 2014). Despite Harriet's expertise and good intentions, however, here are two points she has not considered when thinking about a job description from the perspective of recruiting neurodiverse employees. First, Harriet should indicate near to the job description (if it appears on a website then this ought to be placed on the page where the description appears) that her organization, The ABC Company, is committed to accommodating neurodiverse employees. Second, if the organization has a track record in doing so, then that should be noted there – perhaps through testimonials of current employees.

Selection

Often job descriptions bear little relationship to actual work duties (Belcourt, Singh, Bohlander & Snell, 2014). We suggest that, when you consider writing job descriptions with the neurodiverse population in mind, it's a good idea to be extra careful to ensure that they reflect the actual work performed. That should always be true, but it is particularly important when selecting employees from the neurodiverse population. Job descriptions written by managers should be reviewed by job incumbents (people doing the job) and also by HR professionals to identify any differences of opinion about work duties/responsibilities that surface on the job description and work them out.

Now let's turn to our practical case study. Peter is an employee with a neurologically based disability, and he is meeting with Harriet, the HR manager at The ABC Company, to help her think through challenges in working with employees drawn from the neurodiverse community.

Her goal is to find somebody who can achieve necessary work results. But neurodiverse workers may pose challenges because they may not match the expectations that hiring managers have for how people conduct themselves in an interview.

Consider

- Have HR professionals and operating managers had the training to work with this population?
- Do they genuinely view neurodiverse candidates as viable first-choice candidates, or do they regard them as the candidates of last resort?

Nobody likes to admit their biases. But if Harriet's staff who are assigned to the disability recruiting and selection file are biased, the prospects for success in recruiting neurodiverse people will be slim. Do the HR professionals from Harriet's organization who go to diversity recruiting events attend because they genuinely believe in the importance of recruiting from this population, or are they going only because Harriet has instructed them to do so? Finally, Harriet gives serious consideration to placing Peter on her recruitment and selection team. Remember, it's easier for Harriet to provide Peter with recruiting and selection skills than it is to sensitize someone with recruiting and selection skills to what it means for Peter to live and work with a disability.

12 *Job requirements and job analysis for neurodiversity*

Training and development

It will be helpful for you to distinguish between organization-wide training (this might come about when a new software system is implemented) and individualized training (for a person to move into a new role or to upgrade their skills in their existing roles). Both must be thought of differently when you consider the needs of neurodiverse employees. Organization-wide training is often, by definition, standardized off-the-shelf training. Standardized training has, by definition, typically not been tailored to meet the unique needs of neurodiverse employees.

Harriet was concerned that there is often an expectation that everyone will achieve the same proficiency level at the same pace on a new software system that was to be launched imminently. Harriet thought about the possibility of a collaborative team approach to organization-wide training. She thought to herself: "That team should represent many stakeholders and that could include managers, HR professionals, neurodiverse employees, and trainers. In this way, the team can take a holistic approach to training delivery methods, modifications, accommodations, and expectations." Harriet had sufficient experience to know that disappointment is a function of expectations. She has been in enough organizations to know that training does not take place in a vacuum; rather, it takes place in an organizational culture. She was acutely aware that the state of her organization's culture will be key here, particularly if Peter and others like him need more time to get up to speed than their counterparts. With that thought in mind, Harriet asked herself these questions: Can Peter and other neurodiverse employees turn to their counterparts or managers in our organization and say, "I'm not productive yet; I need more time and or training?" Will managers say to Peter and other neurodiverse employees, "Why don't you get things the first time?", or will our managers work to provide more time and training that neurodiverse employees may need?

For training and development to work for neurodiverse employees, particularly those with learning challenges, it must take place in a supportive organizational culture. How would you respond to the questions that Harriet asked herself? Your response to these two questions will serve as a litmus test of the current state of your organization's sensitivity to the needs of the neurodiverse community.

Performance appraisal

Harriet was thinking about the upcoming performance appraisals. Usually, the requirements spelled out in a job description are the criteria used to evaluate worker performance (Belcourt, Singh, Bohlander & Snell, 2014). However, this time, the appraisals would be different. Harriet has been assigned to work on Peter's performance appraisal and those of several of the other neurodiverse employees who had recently joined The ABC Company. Harriet knew that The ABC Company must practice HR differently to succeed at unleashing the potential of employees such as Peter. The ABC Company was on a journey to change the way it practiced HR.

Here are questions that Harriet thought about at this step of the journey. First, how could the job requirements be modified once HR and Peter's immediate supervisor have considered his unique needs? Second, shouldn't Peter and other employees like him submit their self-assessment, since self-assessments are often submitted to enable a comparison between their perceptions and the perceptions of those managers to whom they report? Third, since this is a journey, can we allow for performance course correction during the review period, and how would that work? Maybe, rather than annual performance appraisals, we might allow for semi-annual, quarterly, or other voluntary check-ins to allow for modifying a job description, since Peter and others are new to their role?

Legal compliance

Legal compliance is commonly understood to mean that "a job's duties match its job description" (Belcourt, Singh, Bohlander & Snell, 2014). However, legal compliance has much broader implications once you consider disability issues. HR professionals must know the organization's rights and obligations to all its employees in addition to those that are particular to neurodiverse employees. All employees are expected to achieve necessary results, but the organization can work with neurodiverse employees about *how* that is best accomplished. One way to do that is to meet with new employees during the onboarding process, review the job description for their jobs, and ask if they need any help to make sure they are best able to achieve results.

Job analysis

Job analysis is key to your organization's ability to leverage the talents of employees with neurologically based disabilities. Job analysis is concerned with objective and verifiable information about the actual requirements of a job. Many neurodiverse employees with non-visible disabilities are underutilized, resulting in their under-employment, because it's often challenging to align them with roles where they can add value. It must be acknowledged here that the challenge of self-actualization is not particular to people with neurologically based disabilities. On the contrary, the vast array of books on the subject testify to the fact that the challenge of self-actualization indeed plagues many people in the general population. The particular problem faced by many people with disabilities in general and by people with neurologically based disabilities, in particular, is that, on the one hand, they have tremendous talents, but on the other hand their disabilities can act as impediments to actualizing those talents. For this reason, much of their talent is at risk of going to waste.

With this in mind, Harriet understood that gathering information through interviews, questionnaires, and observations represents an opportunity for her organization to tap into the unique assets that Peter and others like him offer.

Knowing that she and her organization stood to gain by harnessing this heretofore unrealized potential, Harriet came up with a plan to do so.

First, she would suggest that job analysis be a collaborative effort by an integrated team rather than conducted by one job analyst. Second, she would

14 *Job requirements and job analysis for neurodiversity*

suggest that the team should comprise a specialist with a knowledge of disabilities, a person with a disability, an expert in adaptive technology, and perhaps someone with a background in counseling/psychology. Since there are many disabilities, someone with much knowledge of disabilities could view the challenges broadly and calibrate the job accordingly to the needs of a neurodiverse employee. A person with a disability can cast an educated eye at getting work results based on firsthand experience. Someone with experience in workplace consulting/adaptive technology might have input into the reasonable accommodations that can be effected and are cost-effective. Finally, someone with a background in counseling and psychology would be a valuable addition to the team to interpret any psycho-vocational and psycho-educational tests and assessments to a particular employee besides offering insights around stress-related matters that neurodiverse workers may face.

Harriet thought of using a team approach because she believed that an integrated team would be more holistic and comprehensive and more sensitive to the needs of the neurodiverse community than if one person conducted the analysis. Here's how gathering job information might be different.

1 Interviews. An integrated team as described above will use more holistic job analysis interviews.
2 Questionnaires. Conventionally, these forms would generate data about job duties; the work tasks performed; and the purpose, setting, and requirements for performing the job apart from the equipment, skills, and technology used (Belcourt, Singh, Bohlander & Snell, 2014). By having an integrated team provide input on the questionnaire, she might ensure that the data is more comprehensive and wide-ranging. Here are questions she thought an integrated team might pose to generate disability-sensitive data. If some duties tap weaknesses of an employee with a neurologically based disability, how can these duties be compensated for? If the employer cannot accommodate the weaknesses, then can the role be modified to ensure that the duties are most closely aligned with neurodiverse candidates? Data from such questionnaires would enable a disability specialist on the team to gain insights into how work activities affect an employee with a neurologically based disability. Allowing an integrated team to have input into the questionnaire will yield information that would help Harriet to align the unique talents of Peter and his neurodiverse colleagues with jobs in The ABC Company.
3 Observation. Once again she would recommend allowing an integrated team to observe jobs to gather information. Each team member would see the job with different eyes. These different perspectives would give her more comprehensive job information than if she had only one observer.
4 Harriet wondered if she could get employees such as Peter to keep a diary of what they do. If employees themselves keep a diary, then each member of the integrated team might read the entries and interpret them according to their unique perspectives.

Approaches to job analysis

Several approaches to job analysis are common. Each has strengths and weaknesses. How might they be regarded when examined based on the needs of neurodiverse employees?

The position analysis questionnaire (PAQ) system

The PAQ can provide insights on how different tasks are carried out by a job. Someone who conducts this analysis would rate each job element using a five-point scale (Belcourt, Singh, Bohlander & Snell, 2014). Placed in the hands of an integrated team, the PAQ can be a useful tool, since it allows the team to pinpoint issues problematic for neurodiverse employees. A team would have to review the PAQ first to ensure that it is adequate to identify those issues, and it may have to be modified or paired with other methods. Pairing methods will allow double checking, and that is useful in any job analysis.

The critical incident method

Harriet had conducted job analyses before and is familiar with the critical incident method (CIM). "The objective of the critical incident method is to identify critical job tasks" (Belcourt, Singh, Bohlander & Snell, 2014. Pg. 127). Many job analysts have used it to focus on behaviors critical to job success (Belcourt, Singh, Bohlander & Snell, 2014). She appreciated that the Critical Incident Method is indispensable for an integrated team to analyze the suitability of jobs for neurodiverse employees because it gives a material picture of what someone in a role must do to succeed (Belcourt, Singh, Bohlander & Snell, 2014). As she reflected on the unique needs of Peter and his fellow neurodiverse employees, she thought that an integrated team could look at this picture to determine its suitability for someone with a neurologically based disability. Perhaps the role involves working with a lot of visually presented information such as charts and graphs. If a potential employee has a learning disability in which working with information of this sort is a problem, then an integrated team could offer multiple perspectives regarding this challenge. Is working with visually represented information mission critical? If so, what might be a strategy to help employees from the neurodiverse community? Will role modification help? Can adaptive technology be used?

The CIM method is akin to holding up a mirror to job incumbents (Belcourt, Singh, Bohlander & Snell, 2014. Pg. 127). An integrated team may offer four perspectives on what they see in the mirror. A learning disability consultant may provide a perspective on how to present visually represented information to neurodiverse employees. Someone with a learning disability might have had experience with such a challenge before and may offer insights into how they resolved such problems and also which of their past employers' efforts were most effective.

16   *Job requirements and job analysis for neurodiversity*

Those with expertise in adaptive technology may suggest how technology can convey information in a manner more accessible to those with disabilities. Those with a background in counseling/psychology may shed light on how stressful this challenge may be for a neurodiverse employee and may also shed light on different coping strategies.

Harriet wondered how she could get buy-in from others to attack disability issues in more robust ways. Fortunately, Peter came to her rescue. Peter has been working for The ABC Company for about a year. Although Peter enjoys his work, he has experienced disability-related challenges. Due to his learning disability, his colleagues would make remarks like "Peter, why do I keep having to tell you the same thing repeatedly? That must be the tenth time I've told you this." He also had trouble participating in meetings. He often tried to digest the first point while the meeting had moved on to agenda point number five, yet Peter wanted to grow in his job and the company.

As luck would have it, just as Harriet the HR manager had been contemplating how HR at The ABC Company would be conducted differently, he approached her to discuss his learning-disability-related challenges. Harriet listened and said, "You know, I've been thinking about how we might practice HR differently to help neurodiverse employees to achieve their potential. As much as I sympathize with your situation, ultimately any help you need will come with a price. I will reach out to Fred, our VP of finance, and then the three of us can meet. What I need you to do is to come up with a proposal and present it to Fred and me at that meeting so we can discuss how to proceed."

Peter, Harriet, and Fred met a week later. Peter presented his proposal to have an integrated team (as described above) evaluate his role to determine what accommodations might be needed. Fred said, "Wow! You will need three specialists to sit on this team! Their professional fees will cost us a fortune, and that doesn't even include the cost of any recommendations they might make. Peter, we can't afford all this!" Peter anticipated Fred's response and had found data on employee-retention rates for neurodiverse employees. He replied, "Fred, I understand your concern regarding costs. Allow me to share information regarding employee retention rates. Here's a brief paragraph I found on a website of the Ontario Provincial Government: 'Many studies show that employees with disabilities are as productive and dependable as their co-workers without disabilities, and that staff retention is 72 percent higher among persons with disabilities. That adds up to savings of millions of dollars every year in hiring and training costs'" (Ontario Ministry of Community and Social Services, 2010).

"Well," said Fred, "then I think we may have a persuasive business case for going ahead with your proposal. But I want to see those studies, and I want to run a pilot test to find out if that finding from other organizations holds true here."

Task inventory analysis

A task inventory analysis can be used to develop task lists and their descriptions (Belcourt, Singh, Bohlander & Snell, 2014. Pg. 129). It can help meet the needs of neurodiverse employees by pinpointing exactly what issues may or may not be affected by their neurologically based conditions. We suggest that the opinions of the integrated multi-disciplinary team mentioned above, and of employees and their managers, should be included.

Competency-based analysis

When organizations operate in a fast-moving environment, managers may adopt a competency-based approach. This approach focuses on the characteristics of the people who do the work successfully rather than on the work. The objective is to identify what characteristics make some people more productive than others (Belcourt, Singh, Bohlander & Snell, 2014. Pg. 129).

Many organizations which operate in a fast-moving environment risk leaving many neurodiverse employees behind. As a progressive-thinking HR manager, Harriet is aware of this risk and wants to avoid it. She thought to herself, if it's a challenge for neurotypical employees to keep up with the rapid pace of change, then it will be an even greater challenge for Peter and his fellow employees with neurologically based disabilities. She realized that competency-based analysis might be a useful evaluative tool in her toolkit as she tries to evaluate the compatibility between a neurodiverse employee and a role.

As she thought further about this matter, she realized this method might be useful to help categorize competencies for the neurodiverse employees into one or more of four categories. Competencies which:

- are innate,
- can be learned/acquired without accommodations,
- can be learned with accommodations,
- cannot be learned even with accommodations.

She thought that categorizing competencies in this way would help her to have the essential conversations with Peter and the other neurodiverse employees to determine compatibility with their roles. When Harriet creates a competency-based analysis with the interests of neurodiverse employees in mind, she considers whether that employee is suited to a role at present and also whether that employee may keep pace with the changes associated with that role.

Job descriptions reinvented for the neurodiverse

How should job descriptions be reinvented for neurodiverse employees?

Job title

In most instances, a job title indicates what the role involves, what the status is of the employee, and the level the employee holds within the company (Belcourt, Singh, Bohlander & Snell, 2014. Pg. 130). Job titles would likely not change when written from a disability perspective.

18   *Job requirements and job analysis for neurodiversity*

Job identification section

The job identification section includes standard details such as the location of the role on the organization chart and the person to whom the employee reports (Belcourt, Singh, Bohlander & Snell, 2014). This section too would not change from a disability perspective.

Job duties or essential functions section

This section spells out the responsibilities all the duties entail and the results they are to accomplish (Belcourt, Singh, Bohlander & Snell, 2014).

Much experimentation has focused on this section. Should it list just what people do (activities) or also how vital those activities are to job success, how frequently they are carried out, what competencies are necessary to carry out those activities, and what tools, equipment, or technology may be needed to carry out the work?

Job specification section

This section spells out the education, experience, knowledge, and abilities expected from someone in the position (Belcourt, Singh, Bohlander & Snell, 2014).

The following applies to both the job duties/essential function section and the job specification sections.

As Harriet thinks about how to reinvent job descriptions and job specifications to make them more supportive of the neurodiverse community, she realizes that the differences mostly relate to the duties and specifications sections. First, the multi-disciplinary team should have input into these two sections. Second, these two sections should be viewed as flexible rather than static and that both sections ought to be reviewed by the multi-disciplinary team. She thinks of the specifications and functions sections as platforms for navigating accommodations and role modifications.

Perhaps one statement on a job specification might indicate the worker should possess "an ability to communicate clearly in writing and public speaking." Harriet wonders what might happen if her candidates have a learning disability that makes it difficult to express themselves adequately in writing or orally. As a disability-sensitive HR manager, Harriet is open to the possibility that perhaps this job specification is one she might need to discuss with Peter and the other neurodiverse employees. Maybe this is something that might require an accommodation such as speech-to-text software? How might he and other neurodiverse employees suggest addressing this statement on the job specification? Being clear about what results are sought helps to surface which issues might present challenges for the neurodiverse employees, thereby allowing all stakeholders to have input.

Problems with job descriptions

It's possible that job descriptions could contain certain flaws. One of them might be that it was unclear, resulting in the employee not knowing precisely what to do. Second, a job description that focuses on tasks, rather than results, can become outdated. Third, descriptions that are too specific or narrow could discourage innovative problem-solving. And fourth, there may be listed items unrelated to the particular job, which could result in non-compliance with legal requirements.

(Belcourt, Singh, Bohlander & Snell, 2014. Pg. 132)

We would also like to point out some potential pitfalls of job descriptions for some members of the neurodiverse community.

A job description may discourage potential applicants if the functions and job specifications are focused too much on how the work is performed and minimizes the desired results. That is true for all employees. We suggest you consider how to write job descriptions to avoid disqualifying candidates who may achieve work results but in ways not typical of others in the organization.

We suggest that you consider changes in wording. Instead of using terms like "Ability to express ideas clearly in both written and oral communications," perhaps think about where you might use the phraseology "A desire to learn how to … ." (wherever applicable). If you think this phraseology is not realistic, consider that Google places a great emphasis on this desire-to learn-mindset when hiring people (Globe and Mail, 2017). Certain specifications will be pre-requisites as mentioned above. It's appropriate for you to spell out that a suitable candidate must have the appropriate educational background. However, you might use different wording for other specifications. Let's say that Harriet would like a candidate to know of human resources computer applications. Rather than writing, "Knowledge of human resources computer applications desirable," you might word it like "Knowledge of/ willingness to become proficient in/interest in learning how to use human resource computer application systems." Can you see what a difference such wording makes from the perspective of a potential candidate, particularly someone with a disability?

The first way of wording the specification, "Knowledge of …," has the potential to seem like a formidable barrier because it's worded as an either/or statement. "Willingness to learn/interest in" statements tell potential candidates that you're interested in the motivation and willingness to learn and not just what they can do today. Think about all the essential functions and job specifications in this way. Where can you use this alternative language instead? How can the language you use in the specifications section and essential functions section serve the role of extending your hand to the neurodiverse community rather than putting up walls that screen them out? Finally, you may wish to follow this different wording with a statement indicating a willingness to consider flexibility.

In keeping with our advice above to be open about your rights and obligations (and those of potential employees), we suggest you consider making known your willingness to be flexible with some specifications and essential functions. Your HR department and your legal counsel must agree to the content of such a statement. However, we suggest that you consider a statement of flexibility and inclusion. Broadly speaking, the statement should include these elements:

20 *Job requirements and job analysis for neurodiversity*

1 An acknowledgment that some neurodiverse employees might find job specifications challenging.
2 Making known your organization's openness to consider flexibility regarding certain specifications and functions so long as necessary job results are achieved.
3 That you distinguish between those functions and specifications for which you can and cannot offer flexibility.

Writing clear and specific job descriptions

Conventional textbook prescriptions for writing job descriptions are very formulaic. Such prescriptions spell out the language and phraseology you should use. These prescriptions are understandable, since many managers find that writing job descriptions is a boring process (Belcourt, Singh, Bohlander & Snell, 2014). Many managers are not even sure why they are important.

Here's a different way of thinking about job descriptions. Remember that many people decide whether to apply for a position (or not) based on the language and content of a job description. Often people are put off applying to positions because of the formidable description that leaves the impression that an organization is an impregnable fortress or that the employee is expected to work miracles. So, if you're taking this formulaic prescriptive approach, you may scare off many potential applicants and lose the opportunity to discover otherwise overlooked talent with neurologically based disabilities. It takes time to apply for a position. So people from the neurodiverse community could be forgiven for thinking, "Why bother applying for a position when there's no way that I could meet the requirements?" That's a shame because, when this happens, it means that you've lost the opportunity to attract a potential candidate in part because of the language in the job description. On a larger scale, this means that formulaic cookie-cutter-type job descriptions may erect walls to keep out potential candidates and particularly candidates from the neurodiverse community.

The good news is that job descriptions need not be walls. Job descriptions can be welcome signs instead of barriers. You're likely wondering how to shift from the fortress-like job descriptions you've been writing all along (that may have inadvertently deterred many people from the neurodiverse community from applying to your organization) to welcome-sign job descriptions for people with neurologically based disabilities.

Conclusion and the way forward

Chapter 1 provided a foundation to practice HR differently for the neurodiverse community. This chapter described the importance of job analysis as a foundation for HR and introduced the fictional case study. The purpose of the fictional frame was to provide the reader with a lens through which to view the end-to-end talent management process from the perspective of an organization that is learning how to adapt its talent management processes to integrate members of the neurodiverse community. First, the chapter used the fictional frame to reconsider strategic HR planning. Second, the chapter illustrated how several standard approaches to job analysis ought to be reconsidered to integrate members of the neurodiverse community into the fictional organization. Third and finally, the chapter demonstrated how job descriptions ought to be reinvented for successfully tapping into the talents of the neurodiverse community.

The next chapter examines the job description, the product of job analysis, and ways to redesign jobs to support neurodiverse employees.

Web-based resources for this chapter

- www.job-analysis.net/G002.htm
- https://disabilityemployment.org.au/for-people-with-a-disability/

3 Job descriptions and job design for neurodiversity

This chapter examines job descriptions and job design for the neurodiverse community. A *job description* describes the work to be done; *job design* organizes groups of related tasks or duties. Most HR practice, as the chapter will show, is based on the job description, which is the foundation for recruiting, selecting, orienting, training, and managing job performance.

Welcome-sign job descriptions

Below is a typical job description.

Administrative assistant

About the job

Process daily, weekly, and monthly administrative procedures related to general office duties promptly as per company policy and guidelines. Answer phones and redirect calls to office and field personnel as required. Handle customer calls in a courteous and friendly manner. Process and complete work directives assigned by the Manager for regular work tasks or new initiatives as needed. Support human resource procedures and policies and maintain personnel employment records under company policies. Attention to detail is a must in this position.

Key responsibilities

- Answers incoming calls and directs them to the appropriate party.
- Inputs work orders accurately and on a timely basis.
- Audits weekly timesheets for accuracy and posts to payroll. Ensures expense items are accurate and supported by required documentation.
- Creates purchase orders and reconciles purchase orders costing as required.
- Prepares work orders for billing including costing, accruals, and journal entries.
- Prepares supporting documentation as requested for projects and contracts.

DOI: 10.4324/9781351207478-3

Job descriptions and job design for neurodiversity   23

- Prepares correspondence as requested to customers and employees.
- Prepares quotes and proposals as directed.
- Maintains employee files and tracks attendance.
- Maintains, updates, and files contract and project information as required.
- Completes vendor credit applications as requested.
- Maintains office supplies inventory and orders as required. Assists in the ordering of other supplies when requested.
- Supports safety initiatives as required and directed.
- Provides backup duties to other administrative positions as needed.
- Adheres to all company policies and procedures.
- Abides by all Health, Safety, and Environmental company policies and government legislation/regulations.
- Adheres to the company's Quality System operating procedures.
- Perform other duties as assigned by management.

Education and experience

- A minimum of five years' experience in a general office environment, preferably construction or trade related.
- Post-secondary graduate in administration and management.
- Proficiency with MS Office applications and ability to learn and navigate Ainsworth Software programs.
- A positive attitude and a commitment to customer care and satisfaction.
- Ability to interact with customers and employees in a timely and professional manner.
- Excellent verbal and written communication skills.
- Demonstrated organizational, interpersonal, and time-management skills.
- Ability to multi-task, work in a fast-paced environment, and prioritize conflicting demands.

The description above is for the position of an administrative assistant. The reader is presented with a list of must-haves and what the applicant must do. The message the tone conveys to a potential applicant is clear: either you've got what's on this list, or you don't. If you don't, then don't bother applying.

To write a welcome-sign job description, you must first think about:

1 What are the skills, competencies, and qualifications that a candidate really must have compared to those it would be nice for them to have?
2 What do you need job holders to do from the start, and what can they learn over time? What do you need them to learn in the first three months, between three months to six months, and between six months to a year?
3 Which competencies do you, and those in your organization, have the time and resources to train?

24 *Job descriptions and job design for neurodiversity*

We suggest that you divide a job description into three parts:

1 What do you need a candidate to do immediately? Code in bold.
2 Skills on which the organization is willing to train over a short/medium term. Code in normal text.
3 Competencies you need the candidate to build later. Code in italic.

Below is what a welcome-sign job description for the above position might look like.

Administrative assistant

About the job

Should be able to perform those tasks highlighted in bold from day one. Interested and willing to be trained on skills and competencies highlighted in normal text. Open to performing duties highlighted in italic once proficient with tasks and competencies listed in normal text.

Key responsibilities

- Answers incoming calls and directs to the party.
- Prepares correspondence as requested by customers and employees.
- Adheres to all company policies and procedures.
- Abides by all Health, Safety, and Environmental company policies and government legislation/regulations.
- Inputs work orders accurately and on a timely basis.
- Audits weekly timesheets for accuracy and posts to payroll. Ensures expense items are accurate and supported by required documentation.
- Creates purchase orders and reconciles purchase orders costing as required.
- Prepares work orders for billing including costing, accruals, and journal entries.
- Prepares supporting documentation as requested for projects and contracts.
- Prepares quotes and proposals as directed.
- Maintains employee files and tracks attendance.
- Maintains, updates, and files contract and project information as required.
- Completes vendor credit applications as requested.
- Maintains office supplies inventory and orders as required. Assists in the ordering of other supplies when requested.
- Supports safety initiatives as required and directed.
- Adheres to the company's Quality System operating procedures.
- Performs other duties as assigned by management.
- Provides backup duties to other administrative positions as required,

Education and experience

- A minimum of five years' experience in a general office environment, preferably construction or trade related.
- Post-secondary graduate in administration and management.
- Positive attitude and a commitment to customer care and satisfaction.
- Ability to interact with customers and employees in a timely and professional manner.
- Excellent verbal and written communication skills.
- Demonstrated organizational, interpersonal, and time-management skills.
- Ability to multi-task, work in a fast-paced environment, and prioritize conflicting demands.
- Proficiency with MS Office applications and ability to learn and navigate Ainsworth Software programs.

Can you see how the modified version of the job description is more welcoming in two ways? First, it presents what the employer is looking for in a gradual building-block format. Second, it clarifies that the employer will train the potential candidate.

Job design

Job design refers to the way groups of work tasks are organized into jobs. Getting job design right is critical because organizational structure is enacted through jobs and tasks (Belcourt, Singh, Bohlander & Snell, 2014).

Job design should be approached in two new ways if intended to keep the needs of people with neurologically based disabilities in mind. You may change and or modify a job, but be careful how you do it. How will you know what to change and modify? How much to change and modify? When to change and modify? Which changes and modifications can be made with or without a need for accommodations? Consider these questions when you think about job redesign with the needs of the neurodiverse population in mind.

Second, if job design is to unleash workers' potential talents, one must clarify what those talents are and how they can best be applied. If one were thinking about job design in a neurotypical context, the task ahead might look something like this. Suppose you have an employee with a background in HR. Your task is relatively clear. Their background is clear, and now employee–job alignment is about making sure that there's a fit between their academic background, experience, interests, and that role. Should they work in benefits, compensation, hiring, recruiting, or one of many other HR roles? Job design for a neurotypical employee assumes that they are coming to you, the employer, once they can articulate how their talents translate into credentials that indicate how they might be aligned with specific roles.

26 *Job descriptions and job design for neurodiversity*

But what about someone from the neurodiverse community who has struggled to formulate their strengths into credentials that you can recognize? What exactly are those talents and strengths, and how do you capture them and align them with a job?

As an HR professional, you're likely asking yourself questions such as the following. "How can I be expected to do that? How do I do that? After all, that's not my job, and I don't have the training." You'd be correct. This is precisely why job design for people with neurologically based disabilities will challenge most HR professionals. Doing that is not in the job description of conventional HR practitioners. We suggest that a collaborative and multi-disciplinary-team approach is key to getting the answers right. Job redesign is perhaps best conducted by a team of professionals from multiple disciplines.

Professionals from these disciplines should comprise such a team.

- Vocational rehabilitation.
- Occupational therapists.
- HR.
- Organization development.
- Psychology.
- Management.
- Assistive/Adaptive technology.
- A person with a disability.

Vocational rehabilitation specialists play an important role because "Rehabilitation Counseling has emerged as a counseling specialization and a distinct profession concerned with people who have disabilities" (University at Buffalo, Graduate School of Education Online, n.d.).

The Vocational Rehabilitation Association of Canada's mission is to support and assist those experiencing – or might potentially experience – what they refer to as "disabling conditions." Those individuals are offered a variety of methods to help them accomplish work or life objectives (VRA Canada, 2017).

Occupational therapists can shed light on the ergonomic aspects of job design. A professional with a background in psychology can interpret data in vocational tests and can stimulate insights on job redesign that is aligned with an individual's psychological profile.

Can you see how such an interdisciplinary team could take a much more holistic approach to job redesign? Such a team could bring together an understanding of a person's functional limitations (from the vocational rehabilitation specialist), how assistive/adaptive technology might be deployed to compensate for their challenges (the adaptive technologist), how their working environment might be individualized to be more ergonomic (from the occupational therapist), and their psychological, psycho-educational/vocational profiles (from the psychological professional) with insights into the organizational context (from HR and Organization Development professionals) tied in with an accurate understanding of your organization's business reality (different levels of management). All of this is grounded in the experience of someone from the neurodiverse community on the team. By giving this person a place on the team, you ensure that the viewpoint of the neurodiverse community is represented. It's true there is a large variety of disabilities, and so not all disabilities will be reflected on any team. It's also true that each person's experience will be as unique as they are. However, a person with a disability on your job design team will serve as a sounding board for any job redesign recommendations.

We feel confident in saying that such an approach will lead to a more comprehensive approach to job redesign than if it were viewed from the perspective of an HR manager and or a line (operating) manager. If your organization is a small or medium-sized business, you might wonder whether this approach might cost too much. But it need not. First, engaging members of an interdisciplinary team need not be a lengthy and costly process. Second, some jurisdictions have government funding available to help people with disabilities in the workplace.

Behavioral concerns

Job redesign efforts seek to change a job to give workers more autonomy and responsibility. That is intended to increase worker motivation (Belcourt, Singh, Bohlander & Snell, 2014).

Job enrichment

If job enrichment is designed to improve employee autonomy and give them more responsibility, it presupposes that workers are in the right jobs (Belcourt, Singh, Bohlander & Snell, 2014).

> There are several ways that managers can help in making their subordinates' work more fulfilling and meaningful. For example: offering the employee more challenging tasks, giving them more autonomy, giving them frequent feedback, offering to update training, and assign tasks that play to the employee's strengths.
>
> (Belcourt, Singh, Bohlander & Snell, 2014. Pg. 134)

How might a multi-disciplinary team approach job enrichment from a multi-disability perspective? Let's revisit our friends at The ABC Company to find out.

Manfred is Peter's manager in a sizeable call-center-type setting. His company recruits clients for professional development programs. Peter is in a role that requires him to call on and follow-up with potential clients who expressed interest in the professional development programs offered by The ABC Company. Peter has been in this role for some time. Over time, his role has changed as management has asked him to reach more clients as part of his performance requirements.

First, Manfred would like Peter to use other recruitment tools, such as chat tools enabling them to communicate immediately with potential clients.

28 *Job descriptions and job design for neurodiversity*

Second, Manfred would like to give Peter more authority and control over work outcomes. So, perhaps instead of telling Peter every morning which potential clients to call, Manfred would like Peter to make that decision himself. That means that Peter must become proficient at using a customer relationship management (CRM) system.

Third, Manfred would like to know how to change Peter's job to capitalize better on his strengths. Here's how the multi-disciplinary team might approach such a scenario. Vivian, the vocational rehabilitation specialist, might start by meeting with Manfred and Peter to hear how Manfred would like to deploy a chat tool. More specifically, what expectations does Manfred have, and what challenges might these expectations pose for Peter? Does Manfred expect Peter to use chat one day and make simple phone calls the next? Perhaps Manfred hopes Peter will use both tools during the same day? Maybe Manfred expects Peter to work with both tools as needed, whereby Peter would make calls and respond to chat requests in real time? Any or all might pose challenges for Peter.

Let's focus on one expectation. Perhaps Manfred might want Peter to respond immediately to chat requests on his computer monitor. For some people with learning disabilities or for people who do better at focusing on routine tasks, having to suddenly interrupt their routine to respond quickly to chat requests might be daunting. Some people with learning disabilities find having to express themselves in writing to be problematic, so having to respond quickly, think on their feet, and respond almost instantly in writing might be taxing. Vivian could inform Manfred about how well Peter could respond to expectations. Are the expectations realistic for Peter? Which options are feasible with accommodations, which are feasible without accommodations, and which might not be feasible at all? By having a three-way conversation with Vivian and Peter, Manfred could reach a clear sense of which options might be workable. Once Manfred, Vivian the vocational rehabilitation specialist, and Peter have decided upon which of Manfred's expectations is most feasible, Manfred might wish to bring Terry, the adaptive technologist, into the conversation. Terry could suggest how to best deploy technology to achieve the work results with Peter that Manfred wants. Perhaps Peter has challenges with understanding visually represented information, making it challenging for him to have so much information on one screen. One such intervention might be to give Peter a second monitor; then Oscar, the occupational therapist, could advise how to organize the workstation to make it most ergonomic.

The culture of The ABC Company is also relevant. Perhaps The ABC Company's organizational culture is already supportive of the accommodations we've described above. But perhaps it's not. Maybe one concern at this point is that, if they implement this intervention for Peter, they might have many employees wanting to know why Peter is getting special treatment, and maybe they're concerned about other employees resenting this. How will Manfred respond to questions about Peter's special treatment when Peter expects employee privacy? Those concerns should not hinder The ABC Company from doing what's right for Peter and from accomplishing work results by taking action to accommodate Peter's needs. So, if Manfred, Harriet, and Fred think that their organizational culture might not support the interventions suggested by the specialists described above, then they should consider consulting other experts in management, Organization Development, and counseling psychology.

It's true that The ABC Company cannot re-create its organizational culture immediately. However, it may make great strides at a team level or a departmental level at a faster pace. Remember: The ABC Company need not reach perfection. It just needs to make sufficient progress to make this intervention workable.

The collaborative multi-disciplinary approach we have illustrated above differs greatly from sitting down with neurodiverse employees and informing them that they are expected to perform new job functions without considering the implications. Skeptics might be tempted to say that the process we outlined above requires too much effort and that perhaps what we have suggested is more than is necessary to tap into the neurodiverse population to meet talent shortages. To that we say that the collaborative team-based approach is comprehensive. Precisely because it's thorough, it's more likely to lead to sustainable job redesign. Is it possible that you might have to make job changes later? Sure, but we suggest that, with such a comprehensive process, you're unlikely to be surprised. There's a good chance that any course corrections you make down the road will likely have surfaced as possible scenarios when you went through the consultative process.

What are some ways to design or redesign jobs? The following sections describe some ideas about job design.

Job characteristics

One theory proposed by researchers to improve the efficiency of organizations and the job satisfaction of employees is the job characteristics model. Skill variety, task identity, task significance, autonomy, and feedback are five job characteristics that lead satisfied employees to experience meaningfulness, responsibility, and knowledge of the results performed (Belcourt, Singh, Bohlander & Snell, 2014. Pg. 134).

The explanatory value of this model may by limited for neurodiverse employees depending on the disability. Employees with some disabilities (such as those on the autism spectrum disorder) may prefer routine tasks and may thrive on job repetition. Some neurodiverse employees may crave skill variety but are averse to autonomy. Some employees on the autism spectrum disorder might prefer a prescriptive work arrangement with less latitude. Some neurodiverse employees might aspire to more autonomy but might be constrained from achieving it because they need to consult with managers more frequently than their neurotypical counterparts.

Employee empowerment

The point of employee empowerment is to promote workers to take initiative and have them assume more responsibility and decision-making (Belcourt, Singh, Bohlander & Snell, 2014). For example, employers at a car assembly line saved the company needless added expenses, by cleaning gloves for re-use. In

30 *Job descriptions and job design for neurodiversity*

another example, retirees helped their previous employer find ways to reach out to their particular demographic, resulting in more sales for the company.

(Belcourt, Singh, Bohlander & Snell, 2014. Pg. 135)

Neurodiverse employees might help the organizations for which they work to open up new markets. Furthermore, they and their families have purchasing power. If you work in the travel industry, perhaps your neurodiverse employees might help you think about travel packages tailored for them by making you aware of their sensitivities.

How might you think differently about empowering neurodiverse employees? We suggest that this may be a key ingredient on your journey to unleashing the otherwise overlooked talent of this community. Certain neurodiverse employees might be more limited in how much they may become empowered employees. Let's look at both aspects of how disability might affect employee empowerment.

People in the neurodiverse community, like all employees, should have a voice in shaping job descriptions, job design, and workplace accommodations. And it's beneficial to all stakeholders to listen carefully to that voice. We also draw your attention to the reality that some neurodiverse employees may be limited in scope to the extent to which they may be empowered.

For organizational leaders to create a corporate culture which empowers workers, there are four main suggestions, categorized as "(1) participation, (2) innovation, (3) access to information, and (4) accountability" (Belcourt, Singh, Bohlander & Snell, 2014. Pg. 135).

In more defined terms, that means:

1 Encouraging an employee to oversee their tasks.
2 Fostering a work atmosphere that welcomes new ideas, new ways of approaching tasks, and the exploration of reasonable risk.
3 Ensuring full disclosure and a free flow of knowledge and information.
4 Employees must be held responsible and be held accountable for their work. That means following up on the work that was agreed to be accomplished and earning credibility.

(Belcourt, Singh, Bohlander & Snell, 2014. Pg. 135)

Let's look at the potential implications of empowerment for neurodiverse employees.

First, consider participation. Neurodiverse employees might be limited in how much they can take control of their work tasks. Depending on their disability, neurodiverse employees whom you wish to empower might want to be dependent on other employees. We are not suggesting that neurodiverse employees do not wish to take control of their work tasks; rather, we re-iterate that, depending on their disabilities, some employees might be limited in how much they can achieve such control.

Job descriptions and job design for neurodiversity 31

Second, consider innovation. Some neurodiverse employees may favor routine jobs rather than generating innovative ideas. Examples of this are on the autism spectrum disorder in which employees may prefer to perform routine tasks.

Third, consider access to information. Many people with disabilities are under-employed or employed in junior positions. Many have limited social networks in their organizations and may thus not receive valuable information when needed.

Fourth, consider accountability. Empowerment may require more individu-alization with employees who have neurologically based disabilities than with other employees. Depending on individuals, their roles, and their disabilities, you may have to invest more time in reaching an understanding and agreement. Some people with neurologically based disabilities, particularly those afflicted with mental health issues, may have less control than others over how they relate to other people. Some such individuals either do not control how they relate to others (for example people with bipolar disorder), or they might not have the same degree of social awareness that others have because their disabilities do not permit them to detect social cues. It is more challenging to hold people accountable for their behaviors when they are unaware of how their actions appear to others.

Designing work for groups and teams

Employee involvement groups (EIs), also known as quality circles, are frequent meetings with anywhere between five to ten workers, with the aim of pointing out potential work-related issues and finding ways to mitigate them. The result can be more significant employee involvement within the company (Belcourt, Singh, Bohlander & Snell, 2014. Pg. 138). How might EI's or quality circles be reconsidered?

EIs have the potential to help or hinder the progress of neurodiverse employees. They may give them opportunities to have a voice in achieving organizational goals. Participating in such groups may also be important for surfacing challenges that neurodiverse employees face in performing their work duties.

The ability of neurodiverse employees to contribute to EIs will depend on the organizational culture. Does your organizational culture make it comfortable for employees to disclose their disabilities to colleagues in the EI? How will disclosures be received? Would their colleagues already know about their disabilities (if they are not visible), or would neurodiverse workers have to disclose it to work in the group? Will the recommendations relate only to organizational issues, or might they touch upon issues that are particular to neurodiverse employees? Employees who participate in EIs should receive comprehensive training in problem identifi-cation, analysis, and various decision-making tools (such as statistical analysis and cause-effect diagrams) (Belcourt, Singh, Bohlander & Snell, 2014. Pg. 138).

That begs several questions: Will the training be provided in a manner that's suitable for your neurodiverse employees? Who will conduct the training? Will accommodations be in place for this training? Will a multi-disciplinary team be allowed to provide input in the training design? Will neurodiverse employees have

32 *Job descriptions and job design for neurodiversity*

authentic opportunities to express their disability-related needs as they perceive them? We contend that the answers to these questions should be a litmus test for how well EIs will help your organization.

Employee teams

A team – that is, mutually supportive individuals who collaborate for similar goals – can accomplish an effect greater than the sum of their separate parts (Belcourt, Singh, Bohlander & Snell, 2014).

There are six team qualities that, combined, create meaningful cooperation.

1 The ability of team members to feel they can comfortably offer feedback and input.
2 When team members listen to each other carefully and seek clarification when they do not understand.
3 Acknowledging that differences of opinion will occur.
4 Knowing that the value of compromise and negotiation is often integral to decision-making.
5 Team members should be appreciated for what they offer and their unique skills.
6 Everyone in the team should strive to perform with excellence, pay attention to detail, and be aware of opportunities to do better.

(Belcourt, Singh, Bohlander & Snell, 2014. Pg. 139)

Even a cursory look at the ingredients of a synergistic team should make employers ask how neurodiverse employees can become team members.

What characteristics above might pose challenges for some people from the neurodiverse community?

First, in a synergistic team, the team exhibits an atmosphere of inclusion. This depends upon the corporate culture. How supportive is the culture for people with neurologically based disabilities to serve on a team? Do they feel comfortable with disclosing their disability to their colleagues and co-workers in your organization? If so, then they will likely feel comfortable making it known to the team. If there is such a supportive organizational culture, then there's a possibility that some or many of the team members may already know that they have a neurodiverse colleague on the team (although this will depend on the size and nature of the organization). If such employees feel uncomfortable knowing that awareness of their disabilities will go beyond the walls of the HR office, then it will be challenging for them to feel comfortable about disclosing their disabilities.

Second, depending on their disabilities, some people with neurologically based disabilities may need to clarify what other team members can expect from them. Depending on how much additional clarification they must provide, other team members might perceive the information or requests as excessive – and even strange. That will likely be less of a problem if your organization has a corporate culture that is supportive of neurodiverse employees. Many neurotypical employees must be aware that what might initially seem like excessive or even obsessive clarification might be a coping mechanism to help process information.

Third, consider disagreement and consensus. Disagreement among people is natural, but team members should agree by consensus. Team members must first understand what their colleagues are saying to agree/disagree and know how to reach consensus. Since many team meetings are called on at the spur of the moment, and many discussions take place quickly to solve work-related problems, some neurodiverse employees might have trouble keeping up with the pace of such hastily called meetings.

Here are three simple things that may be done to help employees who have neurologically based disabilities to prepare for, keep current with and participate in team meetings. First, provide them with an agenda in advance. That will help them to think about the topics before the meeting. Second, give them advance copies of any PowerPoint presentations. That simple step may help some of them to participate more effectively. Third, consider using a range of assistive devices. Some might be as simple as recording devices; others might be more robust like laptops, voice-to-text devices (such as Livescribe), and iPads. For a list of 25 assistive devices used by students who have neurologically based disabilities, see The Innovative Educator (2011).

Assistive devices are visible to other team members. Their presence tests team culture and the attitudes of team members toward neurodiverse employees. The visible devices send a signal to other team members that something is different about the person who brought in a device. Are the other team members comfortable with being recorded? Discomfort with being recorded is likely indicative of low trust levels in the team. The second telling sign is whether such employees can bring a recording device into a meeting without mentioning it or whether its appearance must be preceded by a management briefing. If devices can be brought to meetings without briefings, it is likely indicative of a high-trust corporate culture that supports neurodiverse employees.

Flexible work schedules

Flexible work schedules are well-known to HR professionals. They know about examples such as compressed work weeks, flextime, job-sharing, and telecommuting. But implementing flexible work schedules may pose unique challenges with neurodiverse employees. At the same time, the advantages often outweigh the disadvantages.

Compressed work week

A typical example of the compressed work week is one in which an employee works four days a week, ten hours per day, instead of five eight-hour days a week. One common reason for implementing a compressed work week schedule is to facilitate personal medical appointments (Belcourt, Singh, Bohlander & Snell, 2014. Pg. 142). Neurodiverse employees may favor such arrangements if they have

34   *Job descriptions and job design for neurodiversity*

frequent medical appointments. The advantage of a compressed work week is that it accommodates employee needs. However, a compressed work week might not be the solution if your employee has time- and life-management challenges. We suggest that you might wish to consider flextime with modifications for employees with those challenges.

Flextime

Flextime allows employees to choose starting and quitting times so long as they work a fixed number of hours per day or week. Flextime gives employees latitude in scheduling their work if they are present at certain times. Like the compressed work week, this arrangement offers employees the flexibility to balance personal needs and work responsibilities (Belcourt, Singh, Bohlander & Snell, 2014. Pg. 143).

We suggest that you consider flextime from another perspective when working with people with disabilities.

Flextime is usually thought of as an example of a flexible work schedule. But it can also be a mindset when working with neurodiverse employees with life- and time-management challenges. We all have to make choices about what is important. It is true that employers should expect timely arrivals to work from all employees. But neurodiverse employees who are productive and are fulfilling their responsibilities may require some flexibility.

Here's how adopting a flextime mindset might manifest itself.

The neurodiverse employee's supervisor should meet with him or her and agree on a window of time for work arrivals without having to contact the supervisor with an estimated arrival time. The neurodiverse employee need not communicate their ETAs daily; they need to arrive during that window. If that person works as part of a team, team members should be part of this conversation. Give neurodiverse employees the flexibility to work from home at the last minute if needed.

Time spent in rush hour traffic or on a public transit system adds to the daily stress. This is even more so for employees whose disabilities present them with challenges such as punctuality and following directions to a destination. Adopting a flextime mindset promises to be an essential contribution to enhancing a neurodiverse employee's productivity in the workplace by not only accommodating their personal needs (such as medical appointments) but also removing a significant source of daily stress. Employers who adopt a flextime mindset will allow neurodiverse employees to devote their mental energy to producing quality work.

Job-sharing

"The arrangement whereby two part-time employees perform a job that otherwise would be held by one full-time employee is called job-sharing" (Belcourt, Singh, Bohlander & Snell, 2014. Pg. 143). It has the potential to be useful to the neurodiverse population. However, it also brings challenges.

Job-sharing may allow employers to divide a job into two parts: those aspects suited to an employee with a neurologically based disability and those that are not. It is a way to make a reasonable accommodation. Consider using this approach to align neurodiverse employees with tasks to which they are best suited. However, excellent communication among job partners is critical so that their work is complementary.

Good communication speaks to the prevailing organizational culture. Remember that conversations may range from small talk to issues around the job-sharing arrangement. Does a neurodiverse employee feel comfortable disclosing this matter with others? Would the other employee with whom the job is shared feel comfortable with engaging in discussions around disability-related matters? How will you navigate the matter of workplace accommodations such as adaptive technology? Remember, these types of conversations don't take place in a vacuum. They take place in an organizational culture. If your organization does not have the culture in which these sorts of conversations can comfortably take place, a job-sharing arrangement with a neurodiverse employee will be difficult.

Telecommuting

"Telecommuting is the use of personal computers, networks, and other communications technology to do work in the home that is traditionally done in the workplace" (Belcourt, Singh, Bohlander & Snell, 2014. Pg. 144). Like the preceding examples of a flexible work schedule, telecommuting may be a practical option to help neurodiverse employees by providing them with increased flexibility and helping them balance their personal and work needs.

You should consider three issues if you think about using telecommuting with neurodiverse employees.

First, depending on the disability, the employee may need adaptive technology. They would need this irrespective of whether they were working at the office or from home. If they are working from home, the following issues need to be addressed. Who will install and troubleshoot this? Are there particular tools they might need to work from that home they might otherwise not have required if they were working at the office? Do any of these tools need to be adapted, and how will this be done?

Second, consider ergonomics. That is important for the general population and for employees from the neurodiverse community who also have physical disabilities and mobility challenges. How will these ergonomic issues be addressed? Who will assess the employee's home office and make the recommendations? It might be necessary to bring in an occupational therapist or some other specialist to see that the workplace is ergonomically set up.

Third, consider training needs. As an employer, you may be limited in your ability to provide an employee who works from home with training. Can the training be done over the phone or virtually? Your neurodiverse employees might need disability-specific accommodations for training, and it may not be possible to provide that training to them (depending on the training and the nature of their

36 *Job descriptions and job design for neurodiversity*

disability) when they are at home. They may need to come into the workplace to receive this training.

Conclusion and the way forward

Chapter 3 explained how job analysis and job design could support neurodiverse employees. The next chapter centers on recruiting from the neurodiverse community.

Web-based resources for this chapter

- www.duanemorris.com/articles/ten_mistakes_reasonable_accommodation_3 721.html

A Tool for Reflecting on How to Make Job Analysis and Job Descriptions More Sensitive to the Neurodiverse Community

Directions: Use this tool to guide your thinking, and that of others in your organization, on how the job analysis process and job descriptions can unleash the talents of neurodiverse employees. For each question appearing in the left column below, write your answers in the right column. Then compare your thoughts to others in the organization – including the views of your employees who have neurologically based disabilities. While there are no right or wrong answers to the questions, the goal of this tool is to reflect on how your organization's traditional ways of conducting job analysis and writing job descriptions can be changed so that neurodiverse employees may actualize their talents.

Questions		Your Answers
1	How does your organization presently conduct job analysis? Describe the approach used step-by-step.	
2	How could your organization conduct job analysis in ways that will help to identify and capture the talents of people with neurologically based disabilities? Describe an approach somewhat different from your answer to question 1.	
3	How does your organization typically format job descriptions? How is work described and what format is used for the typical job description in your organization?	
4	How could your organization format job descriptions in ways that would increase the likelihood that someone with a neurologically based disability will apply for the position? How could work be described and what format could be used for a job description to let people with neurologically based differences know that your organization is a place where they can actualize their talents?	
5	How does your organization typically format job specifications (that is, descriptions of the education, experience, and other qualifications necessary to qualify for a job)? How could a job specification be written in a way to make it resonate with people from the neurodiverse community who may have followed a very unconventional and atypical path to gain their education, experience, and qualifications?	

4 Recruiting for neurodiversity

The conventional view of recruitment is relatively simple. Once the job description has been written based on a thorough job analysis, HR professionals (and others) source applicants inside and outside the organization. When recruiting, HR professionals will find that their success hinges on how well the organization can attract the best candidates, the caliber of the positions they're trying to fill, and the reputation of the organization as an employer.

By now you've probably figured out that the conventional textbook approach will not work when recruiting people from the pool of neurodiverse talent. You're likely asking yourself questions like "How do a firm's recruiting abilities (and by extension the abilities of the firm's recruiters) need to be different for this unique population?" "Is it better to recruit internally or externally for people with disabilities and how will internal and external recruiting be different?" "What are the unique personal attributes needed for recruiting people with disabilities?" "What makes for a strong employment 'brand' for people with disabilities?"

If you're asking yourself those questions, then you're in good company, because Harriet, the HR manager at The ABC Company, also grappled with those questions.

In this chapter, let's look and see how she dealt with those questions and what lessons we might learn from her experience. There had been more turnover in customer service, sales, and IT positions, and Harriet was tasked with leading The ABC Company's recruiting efforts to fill those positions. She had recently read an article online where she learned that people with disabilities have higher retention rates than other workers. She thought to herself, "Perhaps I should tap into the neurodiverse population as a way of reducing turnover in those positions." Then she thought to herself, "How will the organization's recruiting abilities need to be different for this unique population? What are the unique personal attributes my recruiting team and I will need to recruit successfully from this population? I think we have a strong employer brand, but do we have one for the neurodiverse community, and what does that mean for people with neurologically based disabilities? We have few employees on staff who are drawn from the neurodiverse population, so I will have to go the external route. How will that be different?"

Harriet was overwhelmed as she thought about these issues and felt ill-equipped to address these questions.

DOI: 10.4324/9781351207478-4

Then she thought, "I wonder whether Peter, who has a neurologically based disability, would be willing to help me brainstorm on ways to answer these questions?" She arranged a meeting with him, and she was pleased to learn that he was willing to chat. After Harriet posed her questions to Peter, she asked him if he would assist her. "Harriet, not only am I willing to share my perspective with you, but I also have five friends whom I think can offer valuable insights. Why don't the seven of us go to lunch and discuss the challenges of recruiting people from the neurodiverse community?" Harriet could hardly believe her ears. "You've got a deal."

Peter left the meeting and thought to himself, "Arthur has autism (Autism Canada, 2017), Olga has obsessive-compulsive disorder (OCD) (HelpGuide.org, n.d.), Andrew has ADD (Webmd.com, n.d.), Adrien has Asperger's syndrome (Asperger's Society of Ontario, n.d.), and Darren has dyslexia (Davis, 1992; LoGiudice, 2008). I'm sure that our collective insights will make it easier for Harriet to recruit more people with neurologically based disabilities for The ABC Company."

The next day Harriet met with Peter and his five friends. She shared her questions with them. "How will our recruiting abilities (and by extension the abilities of our firm's recruiters) need to be different to attract applicants from this unique population? What are the unique personal attributes my recruiting team and I are going to need for this population?"

Critical attributes recruiters need to work with the neurodiverse community

Andrew, a tall, casually dressed IT professional, said, "It's important for recruiters to understand that some common characteristics of my autism do not get in the way of me doing my job well and delivering good quality work. My responses to communications from people likely seem unusual to people who are not familiar with autism. Since I was a kid, I have heard from others that I don't look directly at people when they talk, or perhaps I might appear to stare at them. I don't mean to; it's just a characteristic of my autism, and it does not impede me from doing my job.

"What this means for recruiters is that, if I were to meet you at a recruiting fair, you ought not to be put off by the fact that I might not look at you directly or that I might appear to stare at you. Once you can get past that, we can have a conversation about my suitability as a candidate."

"Yeah," chimed in Adrien, a sharply dressed business analyst, "that happens to me too. I'm also bad at making eye contact with people and making small talk. But hey, that's just part of having Asperger's syndrome. It goes with the territory. When I was in elementary school, my teachers suspected that I might have Asperger's, and so my parents had me tested. Once I was assessed to have Asperger's, I guess I've just come to accept 'quirks' like this as a fact of life. However, once I began working, the consequences of failing to make proper eye contact with people became significant. Several recruiters just walked away from me because I was not making eye contact. But I was too embarrassed to tell them about my Asperger's in public."

40 *Recruiting for neurodiversity*

"Really?" said Harriet. "You know in the past I've declined to follow-up with some candidates who have neurologically based disabilities that I have met at career fairs for disabled job seekers because they demonstrated the behavior you've just described. What a shame. I might have lost out on hiring great talent because I did not understand what you've described as possible characteristics of autism or Asperger's. What are some of the other characteristics of people with neurologically based disabilities that I should know about?"

"Lack of punctuality and trouble with time management," said Andrew and Darren in unison.

"I don't think I've ever been on time for an appointment in my life," said Andrew.

"Me neither," said Darren, a 40-something senior manager at a large financial institution. "I found out that I had dyslexia when I was in elementary school. My initial challenge was with reading. Punctuality isn't such a big deal when you're a kid. That changed when I started working."

"You got that right," added Andrew.

"If I may speak for both of us," said Darren, "the point we'd like to echo is that our lack of punctuality and poor time-management skills are characteristics of ADD and dyslexia. Once we get to our destination, we perform as well as our colleagues. It's just that punctuality is challenging for us. That said, we both get that punctuality is a critical workplace issue."

"You're not kidding," said Harriet. "I appreciate that this challenge with punctuality is one characteristic of your ADD and dyslexia. I know that once you are on the job, you can perform as well as anyone else. But I have got to tell you that I think I'd get some intense pushback from the managers if I told them that you rarely show up on time. Not to mention the other employees in the firm. How am I to explain that everyone else has to be on time but that you can show up whenever you please? At least, that's the way it might look to many folks in the firm."

"You're correct," said Darren. "It's not a simple matter, and like all other disability-related accommodation issues it's a matter of finding a balance between the needs of the person with the disability and the needs of the business. Here's what has worked for us in the past. First, we're open about it from the beginning. We make this known at our first point of contact with the firm.

"However, allow me to dispel a misconception that we just come and go whenever we please. What we've done in the past is that we've negotiated acceptable windows of time for work arrivals and departures. So if everyone else has to be at work at 9 am, then we've arranged windows of time to arrive up to 10:30 am. So that means that we're considered to have arrived at an acceptable time any time until 10:30 am. How this appears to the rest of the organization is an important issue, and we deal with it by being transparent about it. I would add two other points. If an employer accommodates us, then we will go the extra mile to deliver top-quality work. Ultimately this is a matter of cost-benefit analysis and trade-offs. The organizations we've worked for have come through with more flexibility regarding punctuality. In return, they have gained employees who put in an extra effort and stay with the firm longer than other employees typically do. As people with disabilities, we'd rather stay with an employer who's demonstrated a willingness to accommodate us than have to go through the hassle of finding another employer and deal with accommodations from scratch."

Harriet said, "Now I get it. So recruiters need to understand that a lack of punctuality is a characteristic of ADD and dyslexia and that it does not impede job performance? So, if The ABC Company will demonstrate flexibility and work out accommodations for punctuality, we stand to gain employees who have an incentive to go the extra mile and to stay with us for longer than other employees? If that's the case, then it looks like some of the critical attributes needed for recruiting people with neurologically based disabilities are being empathetic, being authentic, and being willing to have a flexible mindset."

"You got it," said Darren.

"Great, I'm glad we're on the same page," said Harriet. "Although if I may say, the fact that you don't want to have to deal with other employers when negotiating workplace accommodations for yourselves seems to indicate that many organizations have weak employment brands from a disability perspective."

"Yes, that's true," said Peter and his friends in unison.

"Well," said Harriet, "if that's the case, then now would seem to be a perfect time to ask you for your perspective on the Randstad report on employer branding I sent you in advance. It was only seven pages, so it is my hope you were able to look at it. According to Randstad Canada (a division of an international consultancy), 'The key: your employer brand. Your employer brand is all about what you offer to employees, and what makes your organization a great place to work. Nail your employer branding, and you'll have top talent vying to get a foot in the door and work with you'" (Randstad, 2017).

Building a strong employment brand from a disability perspective

"So, then what makes for a strong employment 'brand' for people with disabilities?" asked Harriet.

Arthur, an immaculately dressed, accomplished computer programmer with an athletic build, had been in listening mode until now. "As someone who's been aware of having autism since childhood, I feel I have some useful insights to offer. As a kid, I exhibited behavioral problems and was highly dependent on routine. As an adult, once I discovered that I was good at programming, my dependence on a routine made me a better employee, with the knowledge and understanding of my employer, of course. So, I would say that the Employer Value Proposition (EVP) needs to speak to the unique needs of people with disabilities." "Your EVP is the promise you make to your current and future employees" (Randstad, 2016).

"Look, Harriet," Arthur continued, "as you can tell from the six of us sitting around the table today, we're all people who have disabilities. While we do share common characteristics, our disabilities manifest themselves in different ways. So an organization can't come up with an EVP for each disability. Rather, an EVP must speak to the common denominators we share as people with disabilities.

42 *Recruiting for neurodiversity*

Olga, a slim, stylishly dressed woman in her mid-30s and a manager in a government department where she's worked since landing an entry-level job after graduating college, joined the conversation. She explained, "I've struggled with OCD (obsessive-compulsive disorder) since I was in my early teens. It's one thing to keep checking that you've put the cap on the nail polish when you're in the privacy of your home. It's another thing when your OCD is obvious in a professional environment. So, from my perspective, 'Know your target market,' is good as far as it goes (Randstad, 2016).

"That said, I would want to know what an organization is doing to understand authentically the needs of the neurodiverse population. As the report says (Randstad, 2016).

"What's important to one group of core talent might not be important to another group. So, has an organization recognized the varied needs of the neurodiverse population, and what has it done to identify those needs?"

Olga paused before offering her insights regarding another aspect of the report.

"Harriet, allow me to explain what 'Deliver your brand experience' means to me (Randstad, 2016). As someone with OCD, I have sometimes stayed behind after a meeting to check multiple times that I did not leave anything behind. I've sometimes stayed up to 15 minutes after work at the end of the day checking that my desk was locked or that my computer was turned off. OCD is something that can manifest itself very publicly in the workplace. Although it does not interfere with the quality of my work, I acknowledge that my obsessive need to check various things publicly can seem strange to people who either do not have OCD or are not familiar with it. So, for me, an organization might have the nicest EVP in the world, but if my fellow employees are going to stare, mock or scoff at me, then an organization is not delivering on its brand experience."

"I can appreciate the point you're getting at, and it certainly takes work to get that sort of organizational buy-in with the EVP so that individual employee experience is aligned with the EVP. No organization is perfect," replied Harriet.

"I take your point, Harriet," said Andrew. "It's precisely for that reason that I place stock in the report's advice to 'walk the walk and talk the talk' (Randstad, 2016). I think the report is right in saying that 'Even if it's not the most attractive truth, you must always present the absolute truth.' I would rather an organization is open about the work it has to do when it comes to the neurodiverse population than giving an unrealistic picture, only for me to find out that the picture is far from the truth.

"If it's true that 'The employer brand needs to be an accurate depiction of the company' for the population at large, then it's certainly true for people from the neurodiverse community like us (Randstad, 2016). Workplace accommodations have been critical for someone with ADD like me. If I were to sign up for an organization thinking that they were willing to accommodate only to find out that's not the case, then that would be a source of frustration for everyone concerned. I would prefer not to apply to such an organization in the first place."

"I can see how, as people with disabilities, your priorities are very different from the rest of the workforce," Harriet said empathetically.

"On that note, I'd like to turn to page 2 of the report if I may," said Adrien. "For me, the key words on the topic of a long-term vision were 'Policies and behaviors which define what employers expect of their employees and what employees expect from their employees' (Randstad, 2016). As someone with Asperger's, I would have several questions about an organization as an employer. They would include: How will the organization respond to my request for disability-related accommodations? (Even though it's true that they are obligated to accommodate me to the point of undue hardship, I would rather not expend valuable time on extracting accommodations.) Will the accommodations be put in place seamlessly? Is the organization authentically interested in people with neurologically based disabilities, or are their efforts to recruit such people simply about scoring diversity points for appearances only? Forgive me for sounding cynical, but I've had some experiences."

Darren, who'd been silent for a while, said, "Adrien, your comments bring me back to the first point on the report. '[An employer brand is] a comprehensive recruiting strategy that positions your company in an attractive way and makes it top of mind for potential candidates' (Randstad, 2016). When I read that point, I wondered whether the company has credible disability brand ambassadors. From my perspective, the most credible disability brand ambassador would be someone from the neurodiverse community representing the organization. That would tell me there is someone inside the organization who understands my situation. It would also tell me I have a point of contact within the organization with whom I can open up to about the realities of the disability experience. If my first point of contact with the organization were another person from the neurodiverse community, that would make such an organization stand out from other potential employers and would make it top of mind for me and others like me. You see, Harriet, as someone who is dyslexic, I have poor time management skills, and I'm often perceived to be disorganized. So, it would be refreshing to connect with someone in the organization who would understand that my poor time-management and organizational skills should not be interpreted as sloppiness or as a lack of commitment to my work but rather as characteristics of my disability. No one would ever think that people who have mobility disabilities were not committed to their jobs because they cannot move as quickly as other people. Unfortunately, the manner in which my disability manifests itself may give the impression that I'm not committed and am sloppy. Remember that it's easier to train people with disabilities to be recruiters than it is to take recruiters without disabilities and get them to relate to the life experiences of people who live with disabilities."

At that moment, Harriet voiced two thoughts to the group. "Ok, I've got it. So what I need to do is to make sure that I integrate neurodiverse employees into my recruiting teams so that they're the first point of contact with neurodiverse candidates. On the one hand, that might be great for our organization's employment brand from a disability perspective. On the other hand, if that's making a disabled employee the first point of contact in the recruiting process, then doesn't that restrict my ability to use external recruiting channels? After all, I can't control

44 *Recruiting for neurodiversity*

who the first point of contact will be at a search firm, a professional association, or a public or private employment agency. Surely we're not saying that I'll never make use of those channels again? Aside from all that, our advertising and social media campaigns are going to have to be reconsidered. So, how will external recruiting be different from a disability perspective, particularly if we want to have a strong disability brand in the neurodiverse community? What do you suggest?"

External recruiting channels

By now we're sure you'll agree that it's critical for all stakeholders to pay attention to the authentic voice of people with neurologically based differences for re-thinking recruiting from a disability perspective. On the one hand, Harriet the HR manager, cannot give up using external recruiting channels such as employment agencies just because she does not have control over who interacts with neurodiverse candidates. On the other hand, continuing to use these channels would mean she would not be aware of the unique needs of these applicants and would have seemingly not transferred what she'd learned in this meeting to the challenge of external recruiting channels.

At this juncture, we would like to offer what we believed to be some suitable ideas that might help to resolve Harriet's conundrum. We suggest that, for external recruiting, the recruiting organization collaborate with educational institutions, employment agencies, and professional associations to ensure that frontline recruiting staff engage with employees who are drawn from the neurodiverse community to familiarize themselves with the needs, issues, and challenges of this unique population. Perhaps the recruiting organization might arrange for staff from a professional association, post-secondary institution. or employment agency to have joint activities (for example, lunch or some team-building and ice-breaking activities) with people who have disabilities from many organizations who serve people with special needs.

There are many ways for frontline recruiting staff at professional associations and employment agencies to engage with people who have neurologically based disabilities. With some imagination, time, and commitment, people who work in organizations serving as external recruiting channels can be sensitized to the needs of those people and can build understanding for themselves, the recruiting organizations, and neurodiverse candidates. Now, let's return to Harriet and her sounding board.

"Among the most commonly included information in advertisements in any medium is that 'the recruiting organization is an equal opportunity employer,'" observed Arthur.

"The problem is that's like motherhood and apple pie these days, and that just doesn't cut it," quipped Olga.

"When I read something like that I get the impression that the recruiting organization is simply trying to meet minimum requirements to cover themselves legally," chimed in Andrew.

"I think that recruiting advertisements would be more compelling if they conveyed the message that the recruiting organization is interested in people like us as employees of choice and that a neurodiverse employee's unique talents will be valued at the organization," said Adrien.

Harriet thought for a moment and then said, "You know, having lunch with the six of you has been invaluable. Wouldn't it help if our people who put together the advertising and marketing campaigns had a similar experience, so our recruiting advertisements were rooted in the life experiences of people from the neurodiverse community? Can you give me a sense of how a compelling advertising slogan might read?"

"How about this?" suggested Olga. "Got OCD? No problem. The only thing we'll check is the quality of the work you do."

Andrew came up with another suggestion. "'We're interested in how you perform when you're here, not how long it took you to arrive.' That tells me that I'm going to be valued for the work I produce and not the time I punch in."

"Those examples are beneficial," said Harriet. "They convey the message that the recruiting organization is interested in how you perform and the quality of your work and that you will not be judged by some characteristics of your disability."

"Exactly right," said the six members of her lunch-time sounding board.

It's well documented that some recruiters are not well trained and may be on their way out (Shamir, 2012). In contrast, Darren noted that "if my first point of contact with the organization were another member of the neurodiverse community, that would make such an organization stand out from other potential employers. If the first point of contact can be important for the general population, then how much more so true is that for people like us?"

Let's listen in on Harriet, Peter, and his friends.

Harriet turned to her lunch-time sounding board and asked them, "How do you think we should adapt our recruiting efforts at post-secondary institutions to successfully recruit neurodiverse students? What should we do to prepare our on-campus recruiters for engaging with neurodiverse students?"

Peter said, "You know Harriet, as someone with a learning disability, I think what we're trying to do here is to break down attitudinal barriers and debunk myths and stereotypes surrounding people with learning disabilities and other members of the neurodiverse community so that organizations like The ABC Company can benefit from their unique talents and so that they can gain suitable employment. That's the goal. Now let's consider how we might go about that not just for our recruiting efforts at post-secondary institutions but also in our dealings with professional associations and employment agencies. It seems like the goal is the same. It's just that we might have to travel down different paths to get there for these three external recruiting channels. Perhaps the six of us might help you to rethink how to approach all three channels, not just how to approach recruiting at post-secondary institutions?"

"What role might mentoring play in breaking down attitudinal barriers and debunking myths and stereotypes?" asked Harriet. "I know that a mentor is a teacher, and that much learning is informal between people with experience and

46 *Recruiting for neurodiversity*

those with less of it. Successful people have often had mentors. People needing help approach those they respect for help. That is called mentoring. Organizations can have planned mentoring programs or else organizational leaders can leave it up to individuals to manage on their own."

"I think that mentorship has a compelling role to play," responded Arthur. He continued, "if recruiters had prior experience mentoring people with autism then they would be familiar with some characteristics and manifestations of autism and come to realize these characteristics do not detract from the quality of work that I'm capable of doing. Had the recruiter previously mentored someone like me before they came to campus then they would not be offended by my habit of not looking at people when I speak with them or when they speak to me. For those without autism, that behavior might justifiably be regarded as rude and inappropriate, but for me, it's as much a part of me as the color of my eyes. Also, when I speak, my use of language is very repetitive. I've come to understand that for people who are not autistic and who are not familiar with autism, my repetitive use of language seems weird. But again it's a characteristic that people could become familiar with through mentoring."

"You know, I think that mentoring someone with OCD would be very useful for the same reason," said Olga. "A mentor would see my obsessive checking under my chair after we conclude a meeting. Many people without OCD briefly check to see they have left nothing behind when they conclude a meeting. However, those with OCD might have to check a dozen times until they stop because their brains do not make connections in the same way as other people do. Mentoring can play a powerful role for people with OCD. After some time, mentors would come to appreciate that those with OCD, obsessive checking is not a barrier to them delivering great work if they are in roles that inherently suits their strengths and talents."

Andrew, who had been waiting patiently for his turn, explained that "anyone who has mentored someone with ADD would know that a lack of punctuality is a defining characteristic of people with ADD. Since disappointment is a function of expectations, those who have had ADD mentees for some time would not be disappointed by late arrivals since they would no longer have such an expectation."

Adrien added, "Recruiting fairs have always been a challenge for me. As someone with Asperger's syndrome, I've never been good at small talk. I get straight to the point pretty quickly. That attribute has not served me well at recruiting fairs and events where it's expected that you'll make small talk about the weather, the price of gas, and other issues before getting into discussions about employment opportunities. Someone who's mentored people with Asperger's would not be taken aback by a blunt and unusually direct way of communicating."

"People think that I have not been paying attention to what they've been saying, as I often have to ask them to repeat themselves several times," mentioned Darren. "It's not that I haven't been paying attention. It's just that people with dyslexia have a poor memory for things that they have not experienced. Those who have mentored the dyslexic would appreciate that I am paying attention to what they are saying and that my poor memory is just a characteristic of my dyslexia. I am taking what they have to say seriously, but my poor memory is a challenge."

Recruiting for neurodiversity   47

"Now I think I understand how mentoring can play such an important role when it comes to increasing the efficacy of these three external recruiting channels," said Harriet. "Knowing some of our managers and finance people I can also anticipate some pushback." She continued, "I'm sure I'll hear comments like, 'We don't have enough time for the things that are due tomorrow, and with all the deadlines and pressures how are we going to find the time to mentor anyone? We barely have time for lunch, never mind this mentoring stuff.' That said, I've heard sufficient anecdotal evidence today that would allow me to deal with that pushback."

At the start of this chapter, Harriet asked these questions:

1 How will our recruiting abilities (and by extension the abilities of our firm's recruiters) need to be different for this unique population? What are the unique personal attributes a recruiting team needs for this population?
2 Do we have a strong employment brand for people with disabilities, and what does that mean for them?
3 How's external recruiting going to be different?

If understanding, empathy, authenticity, and a flexible mindset are not prevalent among your organization's recruiters, then this chapter should have provided some information about what to do in recruiting to make it more attuned to the needs of the neurodiverse community. You've also learned about what goes into developing a strong employment brand from a disability perspective. You may continue to use the same external recruiting channels. However, hiring organizations must work to help organizations who serve as external channels to break down attitudinal barriers and debunk stereotypes among their staff about people with neurologically based disabilities. Mentoring can play a crucial role.

Conclusion and the way forward

Chapter 4 reviewed ways to make a firm's recruiting efforts different for the needs of the neurodiverse population. The next chapter looks at career management as a means to support neurodiverse employees.

Web-based resources for this chapter

- www.worksupport.com/research/printView.cfm/73
- www.thinkbeyondthelabel.com/blog/post/how-companies-recruit-people-with-disabilities.aspx

A Tool for Reflecting on How to Make Recruiting More Sensitive to the Neurodiverse Community

Directions: Use this tool to guide your thinking, and that of others in your organization, on how to make the recruiting process more likely to succeed in recruiting people with neurologically based disabilities. For each question appearing in the left column below, write your answers in the right column. Then compare your thoughts to others in the organization – including the views of people in your organization who have neurologically based disabilities. While there are no right or wrong answers to the questions, the goal of this tool is to reflect on how the organization's traditional ways of recruiting can be changed so that talented people from the neurodiverse community are not inadvertently overlooked due to the unconscious biases of those involved in recruiting efforts.

	Questions	Your Answers
1	How does your organization typically carry out recruiting for jobs?	
2	How could your organization carry out recruiting for jobs in ways that would be more sensitive to attract people with neurologically based differences?	
3	What is your organization's employment brand? (In other words, why do people want to work for your organization? What attracted people in the first place, and what keeps them engaged in the work they do?)	
4	How might your organization's employment brand be made to attract people from the neurodiverse community? What are some ways that your organization could establish itself as a preferred employer by neurodiverse people?	

What to do after reading this chapter

Here's what you should do to prepare for the next chapter.

1 Do you know any people from the neurodiverse community – personally or professionally? If so, meet with them to learn about the issues and challenges they face in the workplace.
2 Identify any neurodiverse employees in your organization who might be suited to your recruiting teams.
3 Look at your recruiting advertisements. What message, if any, do they convey to candidates from the neurodiverse community? Do they give the impression that they are considered employees of choice?
4 Revisit your current recruiting efforts at post-secondary institutions. What do you currently do to recruit from the neurodiverse community on campus?
5 Do you currently have people in your organization who are ready, willing, and able to mentor employees or students who have neurologically based disabilities?

5 Career management for neurodiversity

The typical HR textbook approach to career management places much emphasis on the role of the manager in developing talent. Here's how managers might think of their roles based on a conventional textbook approach:

> Good managers listen to their employees' aspirations, act as coaches, identify their strengths and areas for improvement, and offer them continual feedback about their performance. They also ensure that their employees receive training and are provided with self-assessment tools and information about the organization and possible career paths within it.
>
> (Belcourt, Singh, Bohlander & Snell, 2014. Pg. 170)

Reading that, you could be forgiven for thinking that it all sounds too complicated. If that's the description of what a manager is expected to do for employees who do not have disabilities, then what on earth is one to do for neurodiverse employees? You and Harriet are thinking the same thing.

After reviewing about ten transcripts from the exit interviews conducted with employees who had recently resigned, she noticed a common denominator. They all indicated that the reason for leaving The ABC Company was that they hit a glass ceiling and saw no future with the firm. When she was done reading, she realized that, as useful as the lunch meeting had been, she had only had part of the conversation she needed to have.

"If people without disabilities have left the company because they felt they had no future, then what am I going to do about managing the careers of neurodiverse employees? What are we going to do to offer neurodiverse employees meaningful careers here?"

Harriet explained her dilemma to Peter. "I think I ought to get your friends' insights around career management before I get into recruiting mode. I'm doing nobody any favors unless our firm can offer people with neurologically based disabilities a meaningful career. You know, if I could get their insights on career management, maybe we could become a firm where people with neurologically based disabilities could have meaningful career paths? Who knows, maybe someday

DOI: 10.4324/9781351207478-5

someone from the neurodiverse community could become a manager or even a VP here."

"That's very forward-thinking of you Harriet," Peter said. "However, if you would like The ABC Company to become known as a firm where people with neurologically based disabilities can thrive, then perhaps it might be a good idea to meet my friends at their places of work so you can get a picture of what successful work environments for the neurodiverse community look like? You can only learn so much sitting around a table at a restaurant."

"That's a great idea," replied Harriet. "Let's do it."

That week, Harriet met Andrew at his place of work. Andrew worked in the IT department of a large consulting company. Andrew explained some unique aspects of his workspace. "As you can see, I have three computer monitors. One for my work; another so that I can see emails; and a third for my schedule. It's not unusual for IT people to have two monitors, but I asked for a third one so that I can keep an eye out on my schedule for meetings, appointments, and so on. As I mentioned when we got together with Peter and the rest of his friends, punctuality and time management are challenges for me due to my disability, so the third screen helps to keep my schedule in front of me all the time. The best part is that this is a low-cost accommodation, and so it was a no-brainer as far as the company was concerned."

Harriet exclaimed, "I can't believe how a disability can be addressed with such a simple adaptation."

Andrew then took Harriet to meet with Carol (his HR manager) in the boardroom.

Harriet explained the background that led up to the meeting. "I want to move forward with recruiting people from the neurodiverse community for positions at The ABC Company. I think it's important for us to figure out how we can offer people with neurologically based disabilities meaningful career paths before we ramp up our recruiting efforts. Since Andrew and other people with neurologically based disabilities have had successful career paths here, I'd appreciate learning from the insights of a fellow HR professional. Hopefully, I can take what I learn from your best practices and apply them when I go back to The ABC Company."

"Gladly," replied Carol.

Matching individual and organizational needs

"It takes 'two to tango' goes the expression," Carol said, "and that goes to the heart of why Andrew's time here has been a win-win situation. As you well know, employees have a role to play in career issues, and so do employers. Andrew did the right thing by self-disclosing his disability from the outset. He told us about his autism, and he told us how it manifests itself. From the outset, we knew that he struggles with punctuality and time management, and he also told us that he often does not look directly at people when they speak to him. The punctuality issue has been dealt with by providing him with a dedicated screen for his schedule, so he can have it in front of him at all times."

52   *Career management for neurodiversity*

"That's a very inexpensive accommodation. It seems like a small price to pay for helping a top-notch IT professional manage his schedule," said Harriet.

"Exactly," replied Carol. "The good news is that the rest of the accommodations have been zero cost because they've been attitudinal accommodations, and having the right attitude is free. Typically, one might think that someone who's looking away when you speak to them is not paying attention, but now we know that's not true in Andrew's case. So, we just needed to change our assumptions about what a lack of eye contact means to ensure no one is offended by his lack of eye contact."

"How did you deal with his time management challenges? I know that, in our organization, time-management skills are mission critical skills for our IT people," noted Harriet.

"To your point," Carol responded, "it's true that time management is mission critical for our IT people as well. Step one was role modification. Typically, our IT people deal with a combination of time-sensitive issues like troubleshooting and putting out fires, but they also work on projects that are not time-sensitive such as installing antivirus software, installing phones for new employees, updating software, and updating company-wide systems. Those tasks are not time-sensitive. We made efforts to remove time-sensitive projects from his responsibilities."

"Didn't you get pushback from Andrew's colleagues in the IT department? How did you explain this role modification to them?" asked Harriet.

"IT group-wide education was key," answered Carol. "Andrew, do you want to explain how we went about this part of the process?"

"When I started off with the title of computer technician as an entry-level position," Andrew began, "we got the people in the IT group together and I self-disclosed my autism and the manner in which it manifests itself to them, just as Carol described to you. So really what I did came down to three things. First, I articulated my value proposition as an IT professional. I was able to describe clearly what I can do well. That way they were clear on what I had to offer the group. Second, I disclosed my autism and educated others on what it means. Third, I explained that I needed to align what I do with my strengths and that to start I needed to avoid being assigned extremely time-sensitive tasks. That said, the critical element to my successful career path here has been Carol's ability to balance my needs with those of the organization."

Blending the goals of the individual employees with the goals of the organization

"Thanks, Andrew, for sharing that. You see, Harriet, my role in helping Andrew to accomplish career success here has been to blend his goals with the goals of the organization. To do that, I had to do three things that are atypical for my role.

First, I had to step out of my comfort zone as an HR manager. I'm used to dealing with stuff like people going on maternity leave and issues around our benefits package. That was the first time I had navigated a career path for a neurodiverse employee. I had to wear a different hat as a career counselor. After his first year here, we discussed where he wanted to go and how that could align with the organization's goals. It would not be mutually beneficial for him to be stuck in a role where he was continually fighting time-sensitive fires. As someone with autism, he would find that too taxing. Instead, he needed to shift to a position where he could deal with important projects that were not urgent. In our conversations, it became evident that the vital ingredient to enable that would be more education. I advocated the company to pay for several courses to allow him to shift into a more strategic role."

"You were willing to pay for him to take courses after only one year? At The ABC Company, we only pay for courses after someone has been with us for three years. I can imagine the pushback I would get," exclaimed Harriet.

"Oh, don't worry, Harriet. I anticipated the pushback. So, I wore the hat of an educator to address that. I knew what was coming if I didn't get proactive about educating the rest of his group. Here's what I did. I got the folks in his group together. We did it question-and-answer style. I explained to the people in the IT group that, while we typically expect someone to work here for three years before we will pay for courses, we needed to make an exception in Andrew's case. I explained that much of what he would have to continue doing would be very taxing for his disability. I also explained that we were not doing this out of altruism or sympathy but rather because it made business sense for the IT group and the company as a whole. Everyone knows there is a high turnover among IT professionals. Paying for these courses and shifting him into a more strategic role would ensure that Andrew would stay with us for much longer, so it was a very prudent thing to do from a retention perspective."

"So, you had to step out of your comfort zone, wear different hats and be a different kind of HR professional to act as a bridge between Andrew's needs and the needs of the organization," observed Harriet.

"Correct," replied Carol.

"The company has also benefited in another way because, whenever I meet other people with disabilities, I recommend this company as a great place to work for people with neurologically based disabilities," said Andrew.

"Regarding what Andrew said," added Carol, "doing the right thing for Andrew has given us access to a whole new talent pool that we had never accessed before. In so doing we strengthened our employer brand in the marketplace, not to mention that we've become known as a socially responsible company."

"Wow, you stepped out of your comfort zone, and that resulted in higher retention rates, access to a greater talent pool, and a stronger employer brand from a disability perspective," noted Harriet.

"You got it," said Carol. "We're better off from a conventional bottom-line perspective and a triple bottom-line perspective too."

Identifying career opportunities and requirements

The next day Harriet went to meet with Olga and her HR manager. She was looking forward to this meeting, as Olga had successfully risen to a managerial position, so this was her opportunity to learn how a neurodiverse employee had risen to the ranks of management.

54   *Career management for neurodiversity*

"Welcome Harriet, please come to my office. Susan, my HR manager, will join us there," said Olga.

"You're kidding, you have your own office? I guess that's surprising to me since I'm used to seeing neurodiverse employees in low-paying cubicle positions," confessed Harriet.

"I started off in a cubicle when I landed my first job in this department after I completed my degree in finance and accounting. I was given this office after I was promoted to a managerial position," elaborated Olga.

After outlining her issues, Harriet explained to Olga and Susan she was interested to learn how identifying career opportunities had been different in Olga's case.

"Perhaps allow me to refresh your memory since we got together for lunch. I have OCD, and that means that I often obsess about checking things way more than is necessary. There are two implications. First, it takes time until I am ready to move on from checking something. Second, it looks odd," explained Olga.

"Harriet," Susan said, "I'll be pleased to shed light on how the process of identifying career opportunities was different in Olga's case. Let me begin by saying that it helped that Olga had done the right thing from day one by self-disclosing her OCD. She explained to us that she was obsessive about checking things. So we were not surprised when she looked multiple times under chairs when she concluded a meeting. We were also aware of the fact that it would take her longer to hand in her reports and analysis. It's not that it took her longer actually to get the work done. The issue was that she would check the conclusions multiple times before handing it in."

"How did you resolve that matter?" inquired Harriet.

"Well, after some time we were confident in her analysis, so we just told her that she should hand in the report as soon as it was done without checking it at all. Then, if there were any issues, someone would sit down with her to review the analysis. If she needed to review the report, she would do so, but otherwise the report could be handed in without her reviewing it."

"That's so interesting that you managed to accommodate her OCD at no cost. It was just a matter of being patient and flexible."

"Exactly right," responded Susan. "Now, coming back to the process of identifying career opportunities. We had done a competency analysis, and we had identified the knowledge and skills that were needed for the managerial role she currently holds. That said, I'd like to demystify this process for you. The key was to separate out her OCD from her work. Once we did that we were able to consider a viable career path for her."

"So, it looks like the first step was to de-stigmatize her OCD," said Harriet.

"That's a great way of putting it," said Susan. "She met the criteria for a managerial position according to all the standard metrics. That said, we did make some accommodations on the role itself. To take the pressure off her, we have kept in place the arrangement we've had in place since she started when it comes to checking her work. Also, now that she is a manager, instead of having her check the work of junior analysts, we have one of the senior analysts check it instead."

Career management for neurodiversity   55

"That was such a huge relief for me," noted Olga. "You can't imagine what a load it took off my shoulders, knowing that I no longer have to check reports and forecasts. I simply hand them to a senior analyst and then I move on. Truth be told is that at this point it's more a matter of a formality than a necessity."

"Susan, I get that her OCD does not impact the quality of her work," said Harriet. "OCD is one thing; analytics is another. How did you address the issue of Olga's constant checking under her chair after meetings or checking her computer at the end of the day when she left work? How did you educate people in the department about that?"

"So, we did bring in a consultant who ran it as a casual Q-and-A session. It didn't cost much, so it didn't take much of a bite out of our training and development budget," noted Susan.

"Yes, since then I've never had any issues. No one thinks anything of it when I'm the last one to leave a meeting because I check under my chair. I guess people have just come to accept it," added Olga.

"So what you succeeded in doing was expanding other people's comfort zones? While many of Olga's colleagues might have been put off by her constant checking before the sensitivity training, now it's part of what they are comfortable with?" asked Harriet.

"That's a good way of putting it. We expanded the collective comfort zone to include being comfortable with Olga's OCD and to appreciate that it had no bearing on the quality of the work she produces," remarked Susan.

"I can see that de-stigmatizing a non-visible disability, expanding the collective comfort zone, and a little expense made it possible for Olga to not only feel comfortable here but for her to move into a managerial position," observed Harriet.

Career development initiatives

"Welcome to Bank of XYZ, Harriet," said Darren with a beaming smile.

After explaining her issues, Harriet told Darren and Michael, his HR manager, that she was interested to learn about the mix of career development initiatives that worked for Darren.

"I'd like Michael to give you his perspective on my journey," said Darren as he introduced Michael.

"Thank you, Darren. Let me start by saying that we owe it to Darren for self-disclosing his dyslexia from day one. Without that, his career would never have gotten past first base. Let me shed light on the journey. He started off as a client services representative at the branch level. After some time, he had the chance to attend some of our in-house career planning workshops with other recent hires. That said, it became clear that putting someone with dyslexia through an off-the-shelf training program would not work," said Michael.

"I had one career counseling session with my manager, and it became clear that it would not be possible to talk about expectations for another position until I had much more data about what that position was like. I credit Michael with some out-of-the-box thinking to help me in this regard," added Darren.

56   *Career management for neurodiversity*

"Like many organizations, we have leadership development programs for high potentials. We take people and put them in different parts of the business for four months at a time. That way they get a picture of the wider organization and develop a wider range of skill sets. Now, that program is intended for high potentials who meet specific criteria. We put him through that program, but we applied the same principles to our approach to Darren's career development. So, we sat down together. We identified the three roles he was most interested in, and then we set up opportunities for him to intern in each department so that he could figure out which role is best aligned with his strengths, what sorts of accommodations are needed, and which part of the organization has the culture that can most seamlessly integrate him," concluded Michael.

"You're kidding," exclaimed Harriet. "Someone just suggested that approach to me last week. You mean to say you tried it, and it worked for you and the organization?"

"It sure did," said Darren.

Michael continued, "Together we identified finance, marketing, and sales as the three verticals that were of the most interest to Darren. From there it was a matter of thinking outside the box to come up with the right mix of initiatives to generate the data we needed to make an informed decision."

"I started off in finance, where I shadowed a portfolio manager. I found the role very interesting but decided against it for two reasons," explained Darren. "First, it was clear that it was a very fast-paced environment. It became evident that everyone who works in finance is under tremendous time pressure. As someone with dyslexia, I do not have time flexibility, and that leads to the second reason: when you have a department full of people who are under time pressure that does not bode well for integrating someone like myself. I felt that getting me to fit into finance would have been analogous to forcing a square into a circle."

"So what did you try next?" inquired Harriet.

"Well, from there I went to sales, where I was enticed by the prospect of the money I might earn. I was concerned about the prospect of having to perform under pressure due to constantly increasing sales targets. Also, it's tougher to negotiate accommodations for metrics like sales targets. That's because you then get into the complex issue of how to adjust your salary and bonus structure to meet the adjusted sales targets. So, I decided against sales because I worried about the accommodations that I would need. More broadly, I felt that trying to integrate into a harsh target-driven sales environment would have been too challenging."

"So, that's how you found your home in the marketing department?" inquired Harriet.

"That's right," responded Darren. "When I spent time in the marketing department, I found that people in that department were not as deadline driven and were not under as much pressure. Also, since many of those people have worked in ad agencies and other creative environments, they are more accustomed to people coming to work at different hours of the day. My informational interviews were more productive because people were not constantly looking at their watches, as they were in other departments. Also, it's easier to job shadow someone as they develop a marketing plan than it is in sales and finance. I'm not saying that it is impossible to shadow in the other departments, because I did. I'm just saying that the departmental culture was more conducive to a better experience. It was easier for people to be present with me in the marketing department than in the other departments, where I found that people were physically present but their mind was on something else."

"Wow, so I can see how departmental culture plays such an important role. It's really important to plant seeds in fertile soil," remarked Harriet.

"That's a great way of putting it," said Darren as Michael nodded in agreement.

"I would like to add another reason the culture of the marketing department was a pivotal reason for my decision to go that route," added Darren.

"Do tell," said Harriet.

"I wanted to be independent once I settled into a job. I did not want to rely on Michael to constantly advocate on my behalf. The pressure, stress, and target-driven nature of the other departments made it more likely that I would have to rely on him to a greater extent. That was not what I wanted. I wanted to self-advocate. You can have wonderful self-advocacy skills, but those skills are irrelevant if nobody has the headspace to listen to you. So, here is the critical point, the right departmental culture was critical because it was more conducive to my self-advocacy. It would have been more difficult to have had the successful career trajectory I've had if I had constantly had to rely on Michael to come in and hold my hand."

"Your point is very well-taken," replied Harriet. "Let me see if I have understood the crux of your insights correctly. First, Darren's self-disclosure was key. Once he had done that, you had to wear a somewhat different hat and reach out to different departments to get their buy-in to give Darren the opportunity to 'test out' or 'intern' at the different departments. Then Darren had the opportunity to find the department with the culture where he felt that he could seamlessly integrate and most confidently self-advocate and by so doing have the best prospects for career progression. Correct?"

"Yes, I would say that's a pretty good way to sum things up," said Michael.

"I concur," said Darren.

Fortunately, by this point, Harriet is much wiser, having met with Andrew, Olga, Darren, and their respective HR managers onsite.

Throughout this chapter, we've seen the big payoffs that result from non-monetary accommodations coupled with minor financial investments. Carol, Susan, and Michael have all shown us how they gained by being different kinds of HR managers. Stepping out of their comfort zones and wearing different hats was critical. That manifested itself in different ways. In Carol's case, it meant adopting an understanding attitude toward Andrew's looking away and role modification. She coupled that with a minor investment in an additional computer monitor. In Susan's case, it meant de-stigmatizing OCD and a small financial outlay in sensitivity training. Finally, Michael demonstrated out-of-the-box thinking by paving the road for Darren to find an environment where he could self-advocate, a critical skill for career progression.

58 *Career management for neurodiversity*

At this point, we invite you to consider these questions. Could you step out of the box like these HR managers did? Could you wear their hats? Could you adopt their attitudes? If not, then we advise you think about what the obstacles are. Are they personal obstacles? Are they organizational obstacles? Perhaps both? Maybe there are a host of other reasons.

If you are ready to step out of the box, expand your comfort zone, adopt the attitudes of these HR managers, and wear different hats in the process, then you will likely enjoy the reward of increasing access to new talent pools, improving retention rates for your neurodiverse employees, and realizing other benefits mentioned in this chapter.

Conclusion and the way forward

Chapter 5 looked at career management as a means to support neurodiverse employees. The next chapter examines how to select employees in ways that will improve the likelihood that your organization will be able to tap into the talents that the neurodiverse community has to offer.

Web-based resources for this chapter

- http://onlinelibrary.wiley.com/doi/10.1002/hrm.21570/abstract
- www.amazon.com/s/ref=nb_sb_noss?url=search-alias%3Daps&field-keywords=A+Guide+to+Career+Management+and+Programming+for+Adults+with+Disabilities%3A+A+21st+Century+Perspective

Career management for neurodiversity 59

A Tool for Reflecting on How to Make Career Management More Sensitive to Neurodiverse Employees

Directions: Use this tool to guide your thinking, and that of others in your organization, on how to better manage the careers of people with neurologically based disabilities in your organization. For each question appearing in the left column below, write your answers in the right column. Then compare your thoughts to others in the organization – including the thoughts of neurodiverse employees. While there are no right or wrong answers to the questions, the goal of this tool is to reflect on how the organization's traditional ways of career management can be changed to enhance the career prospects of people from the neurodiverse community.

	Questions	Your Answers
1	What role does the organization and manager presently play in career management in your organization? Describe it.	
2	What role should the organization and manager play in career management in your organization to increase the likelihood that people with neurologically based differences will have successful careers?	
3	What role does the individual presently play in career management in your organization?	
4	What role should neurodiverse employees in your organization play when it comes to career management?	

60   *Career management for neurodiversity*

What to do after reading this chapter

Here's what you should do to prepare for the next chapter.

1 Think about the other hats you might have to wear to integrate neurodiverse employees into your organization.
2 Establish an internship program for new hires and students from the neurodiverse community.
3 Review recent exit interviews. Clarify why people have left your organization. Did they leave because they feel they have hit a glass ceiling?
4 Review your training budget. Do you have the funds for your employees to take professional development courses?
5 Look at your budget. Can you afford to hire subject matter experts if necessary?

6 Employee selection for neurodiversity

Harriet realized that her work in HR would no longer be business as usual.

The next day she met with Victoria for coffee.

"When I started off in HR, I was taught that the goal of the selection process was to maximize hits and avoid misses (Belcourt, Singh, Bohlander & Snell, 2014). I realize that I have to be careful about letting biases and misconceptions hinder the selection process," Harriet said.

"It's true," Victoria agreed. "It looks like your experiences with Peter's friends are causing you to rethink how we should manage the selection process. Tell me more."

"Well, let's begin with initial screening," said Harriet. "I'm concerned that, if we use software to scan resumes to find qualified candidates, the software might reject resumes of people with neurologically based disabilities, who sometimes have atypical career paths. After all, many of our colleagues in the HR field are already concerned that machines are rejecting capable people who do not have disabilities. So, if that's true for the general population, then how much more so when it comes to people from the neurodiverse community?" She continued, "The other issue is that the way we do phone screening needs to be re-thought. As HR professionals, we've always conducted short phone interviews and screening interviews to save ourselves time. However, these interviews pose a challenge for many neurodiverse people."

"That's very interesting." Victoria sipped her coffee. "You've brought up two very important points. As for the first, perhaps we might have a dedicated email address to which people with disabilities and others who think they have atypical careers can send their resumes? That way they won't risk being rejected by machines. As for the short interviews, how do you suggest we modify them for people from the neurodiverse community but still retain their time-saving advantage for ourselves?"

"I think a dedicated email address is a good idea. When it comes to the short interviews, where we do use them, I think that a simple modification might be to provide candidates with the questions in advance. That will give people with neurologically based disabilities the opportunity to think about their responses before the interview. Two other modifications I'd suggest would be to allow somewhat

DOI: 10.4324/9781351207478-6

62   *Employee selection for neurodiversity*

more time for the interviews and also to allow for follow-up conversations. That would serve to take the pressure off the candidates who might otherwise feel that the phone interviews are their only shot at the job and that if they do not perform 100 percent, then they've blown their prospects."

Victoria said, "That's a lot of pressure for anyone, particularly for someone who processes auditory information at a much slower pace than everyone else. I suppose it's possible that pressure might lead people to perform poorly in these phone interviews, causing us to eliminate them as candidates. I think we could make those modifications. We probably have lost some suitable candidates along the way."

Employment interviews

"I think the overriding principle," Harriet said, "is that we're going to need to deploy a wide range of interviewing techniques rather than relying on any particular one. Let's start with non-directive interviews. The classic approach to this kind of interview is to start off by asking something along the lines of 'tell me about your experience on the last job' (Belcourt, Singh, Bohlander & Snell, 2014. Pg. 204). Once again, I think we would do well to provide these questions to candidates in advance. Many people with neurologically based disabilities might feel they've been put on the spot and might feel stumped. More than that, I know that, for myself, if the candidate responds to my question with silence, my instinct is to suspect that something's untoward and to wonder why that person can't come up with something. Also, people get an awkward look on their faces when they're put on the spot, and we often tend to make quick judgments based on what we think a face communicates. In my many meetings with Peter's friends, I learned that there are some people with neurologically based disabilities who have trouble making eye contact when they're communicating."

"I take your point," Victoria said. "So, if making eye contact is a challenge in the regular course of events, then how much more so when they are in a contrived context like a job interview? It seems that, without making this modification, we run the risk of eliminating suitable candidates with this type of interview. I believe we could modify this interview without much trouble. I can see that non-monetary modifications can have far-reaching impact. Would I be correct in thinking that some people in the neurodiverse community might experience similar challenges with situational interviews and that the same modifications might work for that interview?"

Harriet responded, "Yes. Situational interviews might pose challenges for some of these people. However, the problem with situational interviews is deeper. Allow me to explain.

"The way we typically approach this type of interview is that applicants are given a hypothetical incident and asked how they would respond to it. The applicant's response is then evaluated by pre-established benchmark standards based on how successful job performers have answered the questions" (Belcourt, Singh, Bohlander & Snell, 2014. Pg. 204).

Employee selection for neurodiversity 63

"True, that's the way we do it around here," Victoria said.

"Well, there are two challenges," said Harriet. "The first is similar to the challenge posed by some of the other types of interview methods, namely that some people with neurologically based disabilities might need more time to think about their responses. The deeper issue on situational interviews is that their responses are evaluated against benchmark standards. These standards represent what's expected from the general population, not from the neurodiverse population. I've come to appreciate that many interviewees with neurologically based disabilities might not respond to the situations we put to them in a manner expected by the scoring guide. As employers, we expect people to act in a manner consistent with norms of what's become known as Social Thinking."

"What, if I may be so bold as to ask, is Social Thinking?" asked Victoria, looking puzzled.

"Social Thinking is a term coined by speech language pathologist Michelle Garcia Winner," said Harriet, as she gave her a sheet she'd printed from a website. They took a moment to read the print-out.

Victoria said, "According to this article 'Social Thinking is what we do when we interact with people: we think about them. And how we think about people affects how we behave, which affects how others respond to us, which affects our emotions'" (Social Thinking, n.d.).

Harriet noted, "'Most of us have developed our communications sense from birth onwards, steadily observing and acquiring social information and learning how to respond to people. Because Social Thinking is an intuitive process, we usually assume it. But for many individuals, this process is anything but natural'" (Social Thinking, n.d.).

Victoria said, "'Many people score high on IQ and standardized tests, yet do not intuitively learn the nuances of social communication and interaction. While these challenges are commonly experienced by individuals with autism spectrum disorders (high-functioning), social communication disorder, Asperger's, ADHD, nonverbal learning disability (NLD) and similar diagnoses, children and adults experiencing social learning difficulties often have received no diagnosis'" (Social Thinking, n.d.).

When Victoria finished reading, Harriet continued, "My point is that, when we get responses that are inconsistent with expected Social Thinking, we might discount them."

"So, you're questioning the validity of the scoring guides as they apply to people from the neurodiverse community? Is that correct?" Victoria said.

"Yes, I think that there are many such people whose responses cannot be evaluated against the standard expectations for the general population upon which scoring guides are based," said Harriet.

"Ok, so what do we do about this? Do we give up on situational interviews altogether, or is there perhaps some way we could modify or augment them with some other information or intervention?" asked Victoria.

"In a perfect world, there would be someone developing scoring guides for people with neurologically based disabilities," Harriet said with a smile. "Of

64 *Employee selection for neurodiversity*

course, the problem is, that's impossible. How can you develop scoring guides that are valid for all people with all neurologically based disabilities, in all contexts?"

"That would be a big job," Victoria agreed with a chuckle.

Harriet leaned back in her chair and thought for a moment. "Reinventing scoring guides for all interviewees with all neurologically based disabilities is virtually impossible," she said. "So since we can't do that, what we can do is to be aware of the potential pitfalls of the scoring guides we do have. My preliminary suggestion is that, if we come across a suitable candidate, we could offer Social Thinking training if we hired them."

The next day Harriet and Victoria continued their conversation.

"You know, Harriet," Victoria said, "we pretty much run panel interviews and sequential interviews according to the book. In most panel interviews, candidates meet with three to five interviewers who take turns posing questions. Upon interview completion, interviewers pool their rating scores and observations about candidates. Based on what you talked about last week, I understand you're concerned about interviewees from the neurodiverse community being under pressure having to face several people. Could such people be intimidated? But, if so, what do we do? A panel is a panel. You can't reduce it to one person. One person does not create a panel. So should we scrap them altogether? Is that what you suggest?"

"I was wondering the same thing myself," acknowledged Harriet. "I think we need to make it a priority to hire someone with a neurologically based disability for an HR position. With the right training, that person could be put on a selection panel. As I've come to appreciate, it's more feasible to give HR training to a neurodiverse employee than it is to get someone with HR training to understand the life experiences of someone with a neurologically based disability. I see such a person on the panel as having two roles. First, they can introduce themselves as such, which will take the pressure off the person being interviewed. Second, they will hopefully be attuned to the communication issues of people with non-visible disabilities communicate. Many nuances would be lost on people who do not have disabilities. I know that I was not aware of them until I spoke with Peter's friends."

"What are your thoughts about sequential interviews in which a candidate is interviewed by multiple people in sequence?" Victoria asked.

"When it comes to sequential interviews," Harriet said, "I think the modification is pretty straightforward. Whereas a candidate would have three back-to-back interviews in the usual course of events, we could offer to have those meetings over three days. One interview a day. That should place less pressure on a candidate and give the person time to think about responses to interviews."

"Ok, that seems like a straightforward modification. It's a matter of scheduling, and there are no costs involved," noted Victoria. "That said, as you know, technology is playing an increasingly important role in the interviewing process. We've done some computer and virtual interviews, and we've also tried out some video-conference technologies to evaluate candidates. I wonder what modifications might be needed when it comes to using technology for interviews?"

"I think we ought to bring in an adaptive technology specialist to help us with that," Harriet said.

Employee selection for neurodiversity 65

"You know it's interesting. Throughout our entire conversation, this is the first modification that's arisen which has involved cost. Until now, all modifications we have discussed have been attitudinal and behavioral. I have to say it's an eye-opener for me that we could accomplish so much without spending any money," observed Victoria.

Employment equity: are your questions legal?

"Harriet, you know I've found our conversations very informative and enlightening. I feel that we're positioned to progress on this front. However, our entire conversation so far is predicated on us knowing that someone has a disability. The problem, of course, is that it's completely illegal to ask people either explicitly or implicitly about whether they have a disability. So, unless someone chooses to self-disclose, how do you suggest we're going to find out whether someone has a disability or not? That's the piece of this puzzle that's got me stumped," said Victoria.

"I completely appreciate the question. Of course, I understand that it's illegal for our HR people to ask about the existence of a disability. It's true, we can't ask. However, what we can do is make it more comfortable for people to self-disclose. Here are the eight things we can do to make it more likely that people will feel comfortable to self-disclose of their own accord. My research has shown me that the key is for us to become the place where people with neurologically based disabilities would like to work. In short, we want to become an employer of choice for the largely untapped pool of talent from the neurodiverse community.

"I have some rough notes, enough for us to get started, at least."

1   *Hire an HR person with a disability to be involved in the recruiting and selection process regarding the panel.*
    People with neurologically based disabilities will likely favor employers where they will have co-workers and colleagues with interests, experiences, and backgrounds similar to their own.
2   *Develop relationships with disability organizations.*
    Organizations exist to support people with learning disabilities, mobility disabilities, the visually impaired, and many others. Developing connections with these organizations will enable an employer to stay current with the concerns and unique needs of these different populations.
3   *Sponsor disability events.*
    I think that sponsoring events put on for the neurodiverse population is an essential way for an employer to become known as an organization that takes the needs of this community seriously.
    We need not spend a lot of money on sponsorships. We can sponsor events put on by various organizations supporting the neurodiverse community.
4   *Clarify on our website and on all recruiting materials that we are open to modifying interview processes for people with disabilities.*
    That is one of the first things that people should learn when they look into opportunities with us. That will make it easier for employees with neurologically based disabilities to ask for accommodations if required.

66 *Employee selection for neurodiversity*

5 *Modify and adapt our website so that the visually impaired can access it.*
   We will need to consult with a specialist to do this.
6 *Peter should serve as a disability brand ambassador for the firm.*
   Other people with disabilities will feel reassured knowing that someone else
   with a disability has succeeded at The ABC Company.
7 *Cultivate relationships with post-secondary institutions.*
   These relationships should be cultivated with employment counselors and with
   course instructors that relate to positions we are looking to hire. It's not enough to
   show up on a campus once a year for a recruiting event. Besides, everyone knows
   that few job seekers with neurologically based disabilities show up to events for the
   neurodiverse population because of the stigma associated with being seen there.

   I think it's more useful to cultivate lasting relationships with instructors all
   year round. Instructors can be effective intermediaries between ourselves and
   the students. We should also offer to mentor students with neurologically based
   disabilities in post-secondary institutions. Doing so has many potential benefits.
   First, students learn from experience. Second, we gain greater sensitivity to the
   unique needs of this population through mentoring over an extended period.
   Third, students in the mentoring program or summer internships may be suitable
   employees once they graduate.
8 *Ask ahead of time whether people require accommodations for interviews.*
   Job interviews are a source of stress and anxiety. Asking for accommodations
   can be painful and awkward. Asking if people need accommodations ahead of
   time could take the burden off people who might otherwise feel uncomfortable
   asking themselves.

Victoria looked up when she'd finished reading. "You've done some great work
here, Harriet."

"Thank you," Harriet said. "I acknowledge that there will always be some people
with disabilities who will not be comfortable disclosing their disability to us. That's
unfortunate. What we can do is to make as much of an effort as possible to be an
employer known for going to great lengths to be attuned to the needs of people with
neurologically based disabilities and to accommodate them. If we earn that reputation in the marketplace and the community at large, then the prospects are good
that many of these people will feel comfortable disclosing their disabilities to us."

"I hope we can earn that reputation. I do still have some questions regarding
other pieces of the selection process that we haven't addressed. Shall we look at
them now?"

"I'd love to," Harriet replied.

Pre-employment tests

With that, Victoria referred to the notes on her laptop. "How do we handle pre-
employment tests, which can create the basis for possible legal challenges?"

"So, if that's true for the population at large, then I'm sure it must be true for the
neurodiverse population," said Harriet.

Employee selection for neurodiversity   67

Victoria said, "Many types of employment tests exist. Maybe they should write the test with additional time? Can we reasonably ask people with neurologically based disabilities to do work sample tests? We've done these tests by the book, and these tests require applicants to perform tasks similar to, or even identical to, the work performed on the job. If there's a likelihood that someone will do a modified version of the job, then what's the point in having them do such a test?"

"On the other hand, perhaps we should have them take such a test with more time to see where future modifications might be needed?" said Harriet.

"I have to tell you that I'm concerned about 'in-basket exercises,' where participants are invited to make decisions under time pressure. What about role-playing? Will role-playing exercises serve any purpose?" said Victoria (Belcourt, Singh, Bohlander & Snell, 2014).

"I would not even entertain the possibility of asking someone with a learning disability to undertake a 'cognitive ability test' without having a serious chat with our in-house lawyer who knows about this stuff," said Harriet. "As you know, cognitive ability tests assess individual cognition skills such as problem-solving, general reasoning, memory, and verbal and mathematical abilities" (Belcourt, Singh, Bohlander & Snell, 2014. Pg. 214).

Victoria said, "I appreciate you introducing me to the concept of Social Thinking. Now we may have to calibrate our expectations for tests like biodata tests. As you know, in biodata tests, applicants are asked about their past experiences, and the questions relate to how their past behaviors might relate to future job success" (Belcourt, Singh, Bohlander & Snell, 2014. Pg. 217).

"I'm not sure how much I accept the premise of biodata tests for the general population, so I'm all the more skeptical of people with neurologically based disabilities. Also, there's sufficient doubt in my mind that such people, who experience challenges with Social Thinking, may respond to such questions with answers that are atypical, inconsistent with our expectations and outside of our frame of reference. So where does that leave us when it comes to biodata tests?" said Harriet.

"I'm not sure. We haven't even gotten onto the topic of personality and interest inventories. It's accepted wisdom that such inventories are most helpful in guiding individuals in their career planning," said Victoria, quoting by memory from years of HR studies.

"Can we use standard personality and interest inventories for occupational selection and career planning initiatives once people with neurologically based differences work here?" asked Harriet.

"I don't know the answer to that question, but it strikes me as being worth putting that question to someone who is an expert on selection testing," concluded Victoria.

"Yes, re-thinking our selection process for the neurodiverse has far-reaching implications for the issues you've outlined," said Harriet.

Determining the validity of tests

Victoria continued, "Yes, but the issues don't stop there. We also need to resolve how to determine test validity. Remember that few tests have been developed

68   *Employee selection for neurodiversity*

specifically for people with neurologically based disabilities. The textbook approach to determining the validity of tests is that there are many kinds of validity and test validation. I took a research methods course when I was in graduate school years ago, and validity is so complex there are folks who spend their lives studying this stuff. People write doctoral dissertations and hold conferences on the topic. So, we will have to confer with an expert to decide which approach to take."

"I would be happy to look into that to find an appropriate person," said Harriet. She was already thinking about contacting Peter, the neurodiverse employee, who'd introduced her to his friends.

Reaching a selection decision

Victoria said, "It seems that there are two additional issues we'll need to resolve to finish working on how our selection process is going to be different for employees from the neurodiverse community. First, how to summarize information. We've been trained to think about a candidate's 'can do' factors and a candidate's 'will do' factors" (Belcourt, Singh, Bohlander & Snell, 2014. Pg. 221).

"That does not hold true when it comes to people from the neurodiverse community. That statement might hold true for some of Peter's friends whom I met. It might hold true for someone like Olga, who has OCD, and some others. That said, the statement will not hold true for many people with learning disabilities. We both know that there are many people with a variety of LDs who have struggled for 20 years to figure out how to actualize themselves, going from one testing place to another, trying one job or course and the next. So, if people with neurologically based disabilities have spent 20 years trying to figure out what they can do, then it's not realistic to expect that we're going to be able to put them through a few tests and come up with a neat, clean answer that's eluded them for their entire working lives," said Harriet.

"Agreed. In short, my point is that it might be easy to measure what people can do when it comes to the general population, but it seems that trying to figure out what people can do goes to the crux of the challenge when it comes to people with LDs," said Victoria.

"We're on the same page," said Harriet.

Victoria, looking at her watch, wrapped up her issues and questions. "The second issue is to figure out the appropriate decision-making strategy for making personnel decisions for the neurodiverse. That is a complex issue, so I'll give you one example to highlight how this will be a challenge. We've both been trained to think that one question to consider when making a hiring decision is whether the goal is to find someone to fill a job vacancy or someone with potential for advancement beyond an immediate vacancy" (Belcourt, Singh, Bohlander & Snell, 2014).

"Yes, I know where you're coming from. When it comes to decisions regarding a candidate with a neurologically based disability, we've seen that trying to figure out a candidate's potential for advancement in the organization can be more complex than might be the case for people who do not have disabilities. How we figure that out and whether to use clinical approaches or statistical approaches to making hiring decisions are all questions that we'll need to address in another conversation if you're ok with that?" said Harriet.

"Harriet, this has been a very informative conversation I'm glad we got to chat. I'm more than ok with that. In fact, I'd like to re-group and include some other members of the executive team. I'd certainly like to include Fred, our VP of finance; Larry, our in-house legal guy; and some other people from the C-suite. Leadership starts from the top, so if we're ever going to make progress around here we're going to have to get C-level buy-in," said Victoria.

Throughout this chapter, we have seen how Harriet and Victoria have discussed and thought through how important parts of the selection process might be adapted, and modified, to select people from the neurodiverse community. In their conversation, they realized that they would have to do things differently. The good news is, as Victoria observed, that many changes suggested by Harriet were attitudinal and behavioral and did not entail incurring any costs.

We have also seen how both Harriet and Victoria are ready and willing to acknowledge the limits of their domain knowledge, experience, and expertise for the prospect of modifying and adapting certain aspects of the selection process. They have realized that, going forward, they will need to call on subject experts, and that will likely mean incurring some expenses.

We invite you to consider the attitudinal and behavioral changes suggested in their conversation. How do the prevailing attitudes and behaviors in your organization compare to the changes indicated by Harriet and Victoria? Is there a gap between what prevails in your organization and what they have proposed? If so, why, and what are some steps you might need to take to close those gaps?

Conclusion and the way forward

Chapter 6 revisited employee selection as a means to support candidates from the neurodiverse community. The next chapter reviews how employees are onboarded, emphasizing that how neurodiverse employees are treated early with a new employer can shape their impressions of the people and the corporate culture in which they find themselves.

Web-based resources for this chapter

- www.eeoc.gov/policy/docs/factemployment_procedures.html
- https://ofm.wa.gov/state-human-resources/workforce-diversity-equity-and-inclusion

Further reading

- Koser, D.A., Matsuyama, M. & Kopelman, R., 1999. Comparison of a Physical and a Mental Disability in Employee Selection: An Experimental Examination of Direct and Moderating Effects. *North American Journal of Psychology*, 1, 213–222.

A Tool for Reflecting on How to Minimize the Likelihood That the Selection Process Will Be Detrimental to the Neurodiverse Community

Directions: Use this tool to guide your thinking, and that of others in your organization, on how to minimize the likelihood that the selection process will inadvertently be detrimental to people with neurologically based disabilities. For each question appearing in the left column below, write your answers in the right column. Then compare your thoughts to others in the organization – including the thoughts of neurodiverse people. While there are no right or wrong answers to the questions, the goal of this tool is to reflect on how the traditional process of employee selection can be changed to increase the prospects that people with neurologically based disabilities will succeed in your organization.

	Questions	Your Answers
1	What is the selection process for employees in your organization? Describe the process step-by-step.	
2	How could the selection process for employees in your organization be changed to minimize the likelihood that people with neurologically based disabilities will be overlooked due to unconscious bias?	
3	What laws, rules, or regulations might affect the employee-selection process in your nation as regards neurodiverse people?	
4	During the selection process, how can workers and managers be made aware of the unconscious biases they might have so that they don't overlook people with neurologically based disabilities?	

Employee selection for neurodiversity 71

What to do after reading this chapter

1 Appoint a neurodiverse employee to a selection panel.
2 Reach out to organizations who serve the neurodiverse community.
3 Generate a list of events for the neurodiverse community which might be suitable for your organization to sponsor.
4 Convene a meeting of your C-level executives to discuss the status of neurodiverse employees in your organization.
5 Identify someone who might be a suitable disability brand ambassador for your organization.

7 Onboarding for neurodiversity

Victoria said, "I'd like to make a few opening remarks before getting into the substance of today's meeting."

"I'm intrigued to learn more about this," said Carl, The ABC Company's CEO, an immaculately dressed man in his 50s.

"Me too," said Fred, vice president of finance, a tall, well-suited Baby Boomer.

"Yes, I must confess you've piqued my curiosity," said Larry, The ABC Company's crisply attired 50-something Vice President of legal and regulatory affairs.

"You've got my attention," said Charles, a high-achieving engineer in his early 40s who had quickly risen through the ranks to become The ABC Company's chief operating officer.

"Thanks." Victoria smiled. "We hope to accomplish two things this morning. First, to briefly share with you some unresolved matters from our most recent conversation on how to proceed. Second, to engage you and bring you into the picture around onboarding people with neurologically based disabilities. I recognize that it is unusual for HR to tap into your opinions when it comes to something like onboarding. Keep several issues in mind. Successfully tapping into the disabled population stands to prove rewarding for us by giving us access to new talent pools and improving our employment brand, not to mention potentially allowing us to increase our market share among the disabled population. There are always financial, organizational, and legal dimensions to HR, but it is important to consider these dimensions for working with people with disabilities. I'd like to hand off to Harriet without delay to shed light on the outstanding issues."

"Thank you, Victoria," said Harriet as she stood at the front of the boardroom. "First, it might be easy to measure what people can do when it comes to the general population, but it seems you're saying that trying to figure out what people can do is more challenging when it comes to people with LDs. Second, figuring out the appropriate decision-making strategy for making HR decisions from a disability perspective. We've both been trained to think that one question we should consider when making a hiring decision is 'Should the selection be concerned primarily with finding an ideal employee to match the job opening, or should a candidate's advancement potential also be considered?'" (Belcourt, Singh, Bohlander & Snell, 2014. Pg. 223).

DOI: 10.4324/9781351207478-7

Onboarding for neurodiversity 73

"It seems that conventional operating assumptions that might hold true for the general population don't hold true for the disabled population," said Carl. "What do you propose as next steps?"

"We propose the formation of a company task force. That task force would include me, Victoria, yourself, Charles, Fred, and Larry. Together we will meet with subject matter experts to address the outstanding issues Harriet just mentioned and help us chart a course going forward."

Fred, the VP of finance, tapped the eraser end of a pencil in his palm. "What's this all going to cost? If we're going to call on consultants, isn't this going to break the bank?" asked Fred.

"That's a good question," Harriet said, with a knowing look at Victoria. "I know where you're coming from. At first, I also thought that accommodating people from the neurodiverse community would be prohibitively costly. However, in my conversations with Victoria, I have shown that's not the case."

Harriet continued. "I'd like to use the following handout as a basis for our conversation. Please take a look at the handout you've got in front of you. The handout is a copy of a report produced by Dr. Talya Bauer for The Society for Human Resources Management (SHRM) titled *Onboarding Employees: Maximizing Success*. It came out in 2010. I think it represents the best thinking around onboarding today. However, as we'll see together, no mention is made of people with disabilities in general or the neurodiverse community in particular. What I'd like us to do together is to discuss certain aspects of it as if we were viewing the world from a disability perspective. How would we apply the thinking in this report differently given our objective to successfully onboard people with disabilities as part of our overall goal of successfully integrating people with neurologically based disabilities into our organization? Any questions?"

"You're asking us to put on disability glasses so to speak," said Larry.

"Correct," said Harriet. "Since there are people here with varying degrees of familiarity with the topic, let's start by clarifying what onboarding is. 'It is the process of helping organizational newcomers to adjust to the organization. While everyone thinks of making newcomers productive as soon as possible, fewer think of integrating them with the corporate culture of the organization. Failures in helping people fit into the culture often leads to turnover'" (Bauer, 2010).

"If I might add," Fred said, looking up from the report, "the faster employees get up to speed the faster we'll see a return on investment. Hey, from my perspective, as long as people are up to speed within 90 days, I'm fine with that."

Harriet, concerned about what she heard from Fred, put aside a cup of coffee. "Well, it looks like this might be a good place to look at this with our disability glasses on. I think we might have to modify our expectations about that 90-day time frame. I can't tell you what the time frame will be for every person with every disability in every role – or for any employee, for that matter. However, I think it's safe to assume that many new hires with disabilities, especially people with learning disabilities and other neurologically based disabilities, will need more time than 90 days."

74   *Onboarding for neurodiversity*

"Well, if such people are not going to be up to speed in 90 days, how long will it take? One hundred and twenty days, one hundred and fifty days? How long? How long do we have to wait until we see a return on investment by hiring them? We can't wait forever."

"I don't have a specific answer at this juncture. On the one hand, we must modify our expectations on what constitutes an acceptable breaking-in period. On the other hand, we need more information as to what that might be. I suggest that should be a topic investigated by the task force in consultation with subject matter experts. Let's table the issue for now and allow Harriet to continue," said Victoria.

The four C's

Harriet held up her copy of the report for everyone to see and pointed to the page. "I'd like to draw everyone's attention to page two.

"There are four C stages of onboarding: compliance, clarification, culture, and connection. Compliance involves workers being imparted fundamental legalities, or policies, related to the job. Clarification means that the workers know what is expected of them and that they know what the job entails. Culture is about helping them understand what is normative behavior in the organization. And finally, connection is about the necessary people, and knowledge, that the new hire must acquaint themselves with (Bauer, 2010. Pg. 2).

"I'm proud to say that, here at The ABC Company, we organize onboarding with a strategic human resource management approach that the authors of the report refer to as proactive onboarding and, which you will note on page four, puts us in an elite group, since only about 20 percent of organizations achieve this level" (Bauer, 2010. Pg. 4).

"Well, if we're in the top 20 percent of the organizations out there," said Carl, The ABC Company's CEO, "then I guess we're in great shape. Clearly, we're ahead of the pack."

"True, we are in good shape, and we are ahead of the pack when it comes to the general population, to people who do not have disabilities. However, I'd like to surface how we can improve our means of attracting otherwise untapped talent that includes people with disabilities.

"It would be helpful if everyone could please take a moment to review the piece of the report that starts with 'Short Term Outcomes of Onboarding: New Employee Adjustment,' starting on page four and concluding on page six," said Harriet.

Harriet used the next ten minutes to review her notes before proceeding.

Short-term outcomes of onboarding: new employee adjustment

"As you can see on page four," Harriet continued, "successful onboarding begins with the worker feeling confident about their performance, with the knowledge that they are doing well at work. When this occurs, chances are greater that they will feel determined to achieve more. The opposite might be true, too: a person who does not feel confident with their work may not feel particularly motivated

Onboarding for neurodiversity 75

to increase their output (Bauer, 2010. Pg. 4). For the general population, our onboarding process seems to work well. Our onboarding processes result in high rates of self-efficacy in job performance."

"This is the case across all verticals (functional areas) and across the organization chart?" asked Charles, The ABC Company's COO.

"You bet. You name 'em, we can train 'em," said Harriet.

"Okay, so if we're in the top 20 percent of organizations, and we have a great track record when it comes to getting people up to speed or helping them to achieve what the report refers to as 'Self-Efficacy,' then what's the problem? Why can't we just duplicate what we're doing and do the same thing for people with disabilities?" asked Charles

"I'm so glad you asked that question," said Harriet. "You see, Charles, now we're getting to the crux of the matter. Our onboarding process works well for the general population because of predictability and clarity. First, we have clarity on the role that someone is being hired for. So, when we hire someone for a financial analyst position, we have clarity on the roles and responsibilities for that position. Barring some changes over time, a financial analyst we hire today will do the same thing as a financial analyst we hired five years ago. Second, the candidate for the position is pretty predictable. We know that we're going to get applications from recent grads who are 22 or 23 years of age, are finance or engineering majors from top schools, and are in the top percentile of their graduating class. So, we simply take our standard candidate, with a squeaky-clean resume, drop them into the standard onboarding program for the standard job. We know how to do that with our eyes closed. Give us a standard candidate I've described, and we can predict within a matter of days how long it will take for that person to be productive as a financial analyst."

"I know, I went through that program myself," said Carl.

"On the other hand," Harriet said, "the predictability and clarity I described above does not hold true for employees with non-visible disabilities such as learning disabilities. The role is not necessarily predictable and clear. There may well be aspects of the role that pose problems for a person with a disability. I've learned in my site visits to organizations who have successfully integrated people with disabilities that one key to tapping into the talents of the neurodiverse community is for organizations to be willing to modify the roles and responsibilities of a position to match the unique individual needs of a disabled employee."

Larry, The ABC Company's crisply attired fifty-something VP of legal and regulatory affairs, leaned toward the boardroom table. "I guess I've got two questions at this point. At what point do we say that a role cannot be modified and that someone is simply not suited to a role, disability or no disability? When is someone just not cut out for that role? Also, how might disabled candidates not be as clear and predictable as candidates who come from the general population?"

"Larry, your first question is a good one. But it's a meta question and one that is beyond the scope of this conversation. That said, I'd suggest adding it to the list of issues to be clarified by the task force. As to the second question, the other piece of the puzzle that is not necessarily predictable is the candidate profile. Candidates

76 Onboarding for neurodiversity

with learning disabilities and other non-visible disabilities are more likely to have atypical career paths and gaps in their resumes. They may have taken longer to complete their degrees because they had to switch majors to find a fit. They may have had to take longer to get their degrees because they needed to take a lighter course load. They may also have had to receive accommodations along the way, such as additional time for exams and papers and assistive technology. So, given that the role and the candidate for the role are not as clear and predictable as we would expect for the general population, I think now you can appreciate why you can't count on using the same onboarding approach for disabled candidates," said Victoria.

"Wow, how does one deal with that ambiguity and unpredictability? I'm not an HR guy myself, but I know the golden rule of hiring: 'The best predictor of future behavior is past performance.' Well, if that's the case, what do you do with people whose past performance is all over the place?" asked Larry.

"I can't tell you how onboarding will look for every candidate with every type of disability in every single vertical at every point on the organization chart. But we're going to have to make a shift from our current cookie-cutter, one-size-fits-all approach to a more individualized approach to onboarding, one that is personally tailored to the unique needs of individual candidates. I think the key lesson here is that individualized onboarding is a prerequisite to employees with neurologically based disabilities achieving self-efficacy or self-confidence in job performance." said Harriet. "Evidently, more work must be done to figure out what that will look like on a case-by-case basis. But, for now, I think there's value in the paradigm shift. With that, I suggest we break briefly and then reconvene to discuss 'role clarity' – that is, how well a new employee understands his or her role and expectations" (Bauer, 2010. Pg. 16).

Harriet continued. "Now that we're all back, I'd like to pick up with role clarity, which is the second area where I believe we are deficient in onboarding people with disabilities. As the report says, 'Performance will suffer if expectations are ambiguous' (Bauer, 2010. Pg. 16). We know from the report and our experience that 'role clarity is a good indication of how well adjusted a new employee is.' So, if it is important for the general population, then it is even more important for people with disabilities. So, as we've been saying this morning, one key to tapping into the talents of the neurodiverse community is for organizations to modify the roles and responsibilities of a position to match the unique needs of a disabled employee. However, you can't ask someone to be clear on his or her role if that role and the responsibilities have not been settled. I would argue that not only should we be open to modifying roles and responsibilities, but that what flows from that is the need for us to hold off on setting expectations until we've worked through modifying roles and responsibilities."

Harriet continued. "So the third area with onboarding we need to work on about people with disabilities is the area of social integration, the 'third lever of successful onboarding'" (Bauer, 2010. Pg. 16). "I think we can all appreciate the words of the report when it says social integration is the third lever for successful onboarding. Meeting and starting to work with organizational 'insiders' is an important aspect of learning about any organization. In addition, new employees needed to feel socially comfortable and accepted by their peers and superiors" (Bauer, 2010. Pg. 16).

Victoria finished making notes and looked up. "You see, up to now we've been talking about aspects of onboarding that lend themselves to structure, control, and measurability. You can structure a training program. You can make it longer or shorter. You can do it in a group format or a one-on-one format. The point is that we can structure and control it. The same goes for a person's role and responsibilities. One way or the other, sooner or later we can iron out the roles and responsibilities for a person's job. However, efforts to socially integrate neurodiverse employees surface our blind spot. This area goes to the heart of whether we have a culture to support the full integration of the neurodiverse. Not to state the obvious, but we can't control and structure every interaction throughout the company, be it in the lunchroom, the washrooms, the elevators, or at company team-building activities. I know from my experience these informal interactions form a major part of feeling comfortable in any organization."

"Can you elaborate on your concerns?" asked Carl.

"Sure," said Victoria. "I have two central concerns. First, we know that many people with non-visible disabilities struggle with social skills and interactions. During the next break, Harriet and I can share with you what we have learned about what's called Social Thinking, which is something Harriet introduced me to before.

"The report suggests (Bauer, 2010) that onboarding can go smoother if new hires take the initiative to make personal connections with their co-workers – be it during breaks, at company events, or impressing a superior with an eagerness to take on more tasks (Bauer, 2010).

"If these tactics are challenging for many people who do not have disabilities, then all the more so for people who do."

Carl nodded in agreement. "You know, I take your point. I don't have a disability, and I found much of that very challenging when I started in my career. I know people with PhDs who could not make small talk and arrange informal social interactions if their lives depended on it. So, if it's challenging for them, then all the more so for people who have disabilities. I guess one issue we'll have to work on is how to support people with disabilities in their efforts to integrate socially."

"My second concern," Victoria said, "centers on whether our current organizational culture is fertile ground for people with disabilities in general and people from the neurodiverse population in particular. Seeds need fertile soil to flourish. I come back to the interactions I referred to before. We are a diverse organization in every respect. But for people with disabilities, we're behind where we should be. I worry about how many of our people, at all levels of the organization chart, might respond to learning that someone has obsessive-compulsive disorder, Asperger's, a learning disability, or any other non-visible disability. Most of our employees are not equipped to handle a scenario where someone discloses a non-visible disability to them at work. I'm not suggesting that the majority of our employees are prejudiced. I think that, for most people in this company, having a colleague

78　*Onboarding for neurodiversity*

disclose their disability to them at work is outside their frame of reference and comfort zone."

Carl's expression grew thoughtful. "So, what do we do about that? If HR folks like you are struggling with this, then how can we expect everyone else to get it right? Does that mean that we don't have the organizational culture necessary to integrate people with neurologically based disabilities?"

When she heard those words, Victoria knew that she'd got Carl to conclude that The ABC Company's culture was inadequate from a disability perspective. "Your point is well-taken, and it's a good segue into the fourth aspect of onboarding mentioned in the report: 'Knowledge of, and fit within, an organizational culture is the fourth aspect of onboarding. Every company has a unique culture, so helping new hires navigate that culture and their place within it are essential' (Bauer, 2010). I think the point I'm trying to get to is that, for an employee to get beyond basic self-efficacy, onboarding must take place in a supportive organizational culture. If not, then we risk the possibility of having employees who are proficient in their work but just don't fit in the organization."

"I think," began Carl, "where we're going with this is that we're going to need to overhaul our culture to provide a fertile organizational culture for the neurodiverse when they get here. Are we on the same page?"

"Indeed, we are," said Victoria.

Fred looked somewhat puzzled. "Pardon my ignorance. But what may I ask happens during the onboarding process? I think it would help me if I could have a picture of what goes on because right now this is very abstract for me."

What happens during onboarding?

Harriet said, "Please make your way to page nine of the report. I think the following aptly describes what we try to do. The overall aim of recruitment, it says, ought to be to guide them to 'the next step – selection' (Bauer, 2010. Pg. 9). Once this is accomplished, it's then on to assisting them in fitting into the organizational environment and getting acquainted with 'organizational insiders and stakeholders' (Bauer, 2010). So while the process of recruitment supplies information, new hires also benefit from knowing what will be expected from them (Bauer, 2010). As we discussed earlier, one of the challenges we face with employees who have neurologically based disabilities is that of expectations. As we've said, employers need to hold off on setting job-performance expectations until working through modifying roles and responsibilities. Another step in our onboarding process is our efforts to provide Realistic Job Previews (RJPs). We do try to provide Realistic Job Previews, outlining the details of the work required and expected, as well as information about the company culture (Bauer, 2010). We think that RJPs have the potential to play a critical role in the success of employees with neurologically based disabilities. Our current thinking is that the RJP would be the first opportunity for a disabled candidate to get a snapshot of what the position entails and to start a dialog about if and how the role might need to be modified."

Onboarding for neurodiversity 79

Harriet sipped her water. "I know that, for some of you, what I have just said will reinforce the question that was raised earlier about how far we go when it comes to modifying positions and at what point we simply say that someone is not suited to a position. I'd like to put that on hold for now so that we can continue to cover ground."

Harriet continued. "Once we have hired someone, we then put them through an orientation. As we all know, most orientation programs are training programs that familiarize new workers with many aspects of the organization's work rules, policies, procedures, benefit plans, and much more. As mentioned on the page you have in front of you, we make use of discussions, lectures, and written materials and will soon move much of this online. We already make use of computer-based information systems and the company intranet to help support new employees. When it comes to deploying these tools for employees with disabilities, some tools will fit better for some people than for others. We must figure out the optimum blend of tools and modifications that might be necessary. I think we're sufficiently far along in today's meeting that it will not surprise you when I say that those modifications and adaptations for the disabled will need to be made on a case-by-case basis in consultation with people who are subject matter experts. Please direct your attention to page ten of the report so I may refer to some of the support tools and processes we use."

Support tools and processes

Harriet continued, "I'd like to continue to touch on some tools and processes we use and to share with you some initial thoughts about how to adapt them to people with disabilities. The 'written onboarding plan' referred to in the report is something we currently make use of. This is 'a formal document, or roadmap, that outlines the specific timeline, goals, responsibilities, and support available to new hires' (Bauer, 2010. Pg. 21). I think that, for neurodiverse employees, it might be more appropriate to talk about a written onboarding plan that is subject to modification as needed."

"I'm with you on that," said Victoria. "I doubt that a written onboarding plan would have any merit without consulting a multi-disciplinary team first."

"The second tool in our toolkit," Harriet said, "are stakeholder meetings. We are consistent with the way report describes it: 'Many stakeholders should be involved in those onboarding meetings, and the schedule should identify who is involved and at what point in time' (Bauer, 2010). However, I think to have stakeholder meetings for employees with disabilities, clearly all stakeholders must be briefed on the unique needs of that employee. That takes us back to the matter of organizational culture and comfort zones we touched upon before. For stakeholder meetings to be productive for employees with neurologically based disabilities, disabled employees must be comfortable disclosing their disabilities to all the stakeholders concerned, and many stakeholders may have to expand their comfort zone to include discussing disability issues. I should add that we have experimented with online onboarding systems. If we are to use online onboarding

80 *Onboarding for neurodiversity*

for employees from the neurodiverse community, then I envisage having to consult with an adaptive technology specialist to make necessary modifications and adaptations."

Coaching and support

Harriet turned a page in her notes. "I'd like to draw attention to some vulnerabilities when it comes to our use of mentors and training. The report put it well on page 11, when it describes mentors as 'similar resource to help new employees learn the ropes. A mentor can teach new employees about the organization, offer advice, help with job instruction and provide support in social and political terms'" (Bauer, 2010).

"I'm sure everyone in the room has had at least one mentor," Harriet continued, "and the benefits of mentorship are well documented. The concern is how well our existing mentors can mentor employees with disabilities, since none have disabilities themselves, to the best of my knowledge. Here are some questions I have concerning the use of mentors who do not have disabilities to mentor neurodiverse employees. Are the existing mentors relevant? If so, is mentoring neurodiverse employees within their comfort zone, and do they have the soft skills to do so? We might have to put each of the mentors through specific training to enable them to work with neurodiverse employees. I don't have all the answers, but these strike me as some questions that must be asked before we ask mentors to mentor people with disabilities."

"It seems that this is a circular problem," Carl observed. "We have not made a concerted effort to hire and integrate people with disabilities in the past, and so now we do not have mentors with disabilities. You can't have mentors with neurologically based disabilities until you have hired and integrated the employees with neurologically based disabilities, but you're less likely to hire successfully and integrate people with disabilities if you don't have people to mentor them."

"Right, and we're going to need to do a lot of work to figure that out," said Harriet.

Feedback tools

Harriet lifted up her copy of the report. "I refer you to page 13, as I'd like to take a few moments to touch upon the issue of feedback tools. 'New employees often make missteps and may find it challenging to understand and interpret positive or negative reactions they receive from co-workers' (Bauer, 2010). If this is a challenge for people without disabilities, then I can just imagine how challenging it must be for people with disabilities such as Asperger's and any personality disorder or non-visible disability who find it a challenge to understand daily verbal and nonverbal communication. All this means that we're going to need to rethink how we deploy two conventional approaches to employee feedback, namely performance appraisals and 360-degree feedback in addition to employee-initiated information and feedback seeking."

Onboarding for neurodiversity 81

"Let me guess, those are going to get turned on their heads as well?" said Fred.

"I would not say turned on their heads," Harriet remarked, "but rather re-examined to optimize efficacy. Let's look at one of the supposed benefits of the 360-degree feedback to illustrate the point. 'The benefit of the 360-degree feedback is that it helps new employees understand how others view them' (Bauer, 2010). Well, Fred, what do you suppose might be the validity of co-worker's perceptions if they are not aware of the fact that some behavior they observe might be attributable to a disability? If the person being commented on has a learning disability, then how helpful is it for us to have ten colleagues tell us he does not get instructions the first time around? I'm not suggesting this tool ought to be scrapped, but only that much re-thinking will have to go into using a tool like this if it's going to be useful, valid, and perhaps fair to employees with disabilities."

"Point taken," said Fred.

"When it comes to employee-initiated information and feedback seeking, I think we must revisit our expectations. The report on page 13 offers a standard textbook approach on this matter: 'As time passes, employees should start asking more questions of supervisors about expectations and evaluation, but they may be reluctant to do so if they believe such questioning will reveal their weaknesses' (Bauer, 2010). As I said before, we're going to need to revisit our organizational culture holistically to ensure that it's supportive of people with disabilities. I hope that with time, as our organizational culture changes, people with disabilities will feel comfortable with pro-actively seeking feedback even at the risk of revealing their weaknesses."

"Harriet, your hopes are noble," said Fred. "That said, I would like to direct my comments to Victoria. Victoria, how do we ensure that this move to include people with disabilities does not open a Pandora's box of people who will try anything to get accommodation at all cost even when they do not need it? How do we know that every Tom, Dick, and Harry isn't going to come along with a litany of excuses and sob stories as to why they should get accommodations? If that happens, before long you and Harriet will spend your entire day dealing with disability issues. Not to mention the cost. Forgive me for mentioning the cost issue, but I am the finance executive here."

Victoria, who had been listening attentively, said, "Fred, I understand your concerns. For now, let me make the following points. There is a moral case and a business case for integrating people with disabilities into our organization. From a business perspective, it is clear to me that there is an ROI here. I can show you the data and statistics some other time. As to your concern that we will be flooded with an army of disability fraudsters, there is no precedent for that in any organization Harriet visited or spoke to by phone. In general, I'm not aware of any organization that decided to be proactive about integrating disabled employees where that has happened."

"Well, that's a relief to know," said Fred.

Larry said, glancing at his watch, "I want to know if and how any of this exposes us to legal liability. It is good that we want to do the right thing, but we need to

82 *Onboarding for neurodiversity*

make sure that we don't get sued. Let's not kid ourselves. There is no shortage of people out there who'd love to take us to the cleaners."

Fred looked up. "Victoria, you know me. So, we can talk all day about a moral case. But for me, it comes down to money. I have two key concerns. Concern number one is ROI, and number two is cost containment."

"I'm the operations guy here," said Charles, "So I'm going to share with you one of my favorite expressions from Peter Drucker, 'Management is doing things right; leadership is doing the right things' (BrainyQuote.com, n.d.). Victoria, I'm with you so far, but I need to see more detail about how this effort will work. I need to look at details, plans, action steps, time frames, and numbers. Make me a proposal."

"Victoria and Harriet," Carl said, "Can you please look into the details around the subject experts we'd confer with?"

"Sure," said Victoria.

In this chapter, Harriet and Victoria were not only faced with the challenge of thinking through onboarding from a disability perspective but also how to gain buy-in from the key decision-makers at The ABC Company.

As you can tell from this chapter, getting buy-in from key decision-makers is a prerequisite for your organization to make the most of disabled workers. We invite you to reflect on how the key decision-makers in your organization would have responded to the meeting with Victoria and Harriet. Substitute the names of your key people for Carl, Fred, Larry, and Charles. Notwithstanding the concerns these four people raised along the way, if you think that a meeting in your organization would have concluded in the same way, then the future bodes well. If at a minimum a meeting at your organization would not have resulted positively, then that's a troubling sign. If that is the case, why would it turn out that way? What are the individual, organizational, financial, and attitudinal barriers in the way of approving such a task force to develop a proposal to improve HR practices with disabled workers?

Throughout this chapter, we have seen how Harriet and Victoria articulated the need for modifying expectations to improve ways to tap into the disabled population. They acknowledged that, for working with disabled candidates, they cannot count on the predictability and clarity of the candidates' resumes and track records that they have always been able to count on for the general population. Harriet and Victoria understand that predictability and clarity are a thing of the past and that they will need to embrace uncertainty and ambiguity for the candidates they'll be working with.

These two HR professionals understand that they can no longer take comfort in the golden rule of hiring that "The best predictor of future behavior is past performance." For employees with neurologically based disabilities, who may have had a work history that does not demonstrate a consistent track record of success, there may be a need to focus on the willingness to perform. The HR professionals in this chapter have also embraced a paradigm shift away from their one-size-fits-all approach to onboarding to a more individualized approach.

We also saw how Harriet and Victoria are bold enough to acknowledge their organization's weaknesses. They are wise enough to know that many aspects of organizational life cannot be measured, structured, and controlled and that the imperative is to create an organizational culture that is conducive to people with

Onboarding for neurodiversity 83

disabilities. They know that at the root of the troubling current organizational culture are the limits of individual employees' comfort zones. Expanding their employees' comfort zones will be the key to a supportive organizational culture. Overhauling their organizational culture will be a daunting undertaking, but they also know that The ABC Company must attempt to do so if the organization is to become a place where employees with neurologically based disabilities can flourish. They dare to acknowledge that their company's inability to integrate people with disabilities in the past leaves it with a dilemma regarding how to mentor the neurodiverse employees of the future. Finally, they acknowledge that they cannot count on feedback tools used in the past. They will likely have to re-examine how the company uses its 360-degree feedback tool. They also know that in the current organizational culture, they cannot bank on neurodiverse employees initiating requests for feedback to the same extent they can from employees who do not have disabilities.

We invite you to consider the attitudinal changes and paradigm shifts that you've read about in this chapter. Are you willing to suspend your expectations for working with neurodiverse employees? Do you cling to the predictability and clarity of the past, or are you ready to embrace uncertainty and ambiguity? Are you and your organization stuck in obsolete paradigms, or are you willing to embrace a paradigm shift in an individualized approach to onboarding? If you're not ready to make the change, why not? What and or who might hold you and your organization back?

We also invite you to think about your organization's vulnerabilities. Do you know what they are, and are you and the key stakeholders comfortable with acknowledging them? Is your organization's current culture conducive to all aspects of onboarding the neurodiverse mentioned in this chapter? What about your employees' comfort zones for working with disabled colleagues? We suggest it would be helpful for you to ask yourself these questions. How would the majority of people in your organization respond if a colleague told them they have a neurologically based disability of some sort? If you think that most would be comfortable with it, then you and your organization may well be in good shape. If not, then maybe you face a situation similar to that of Victoria and Harriet, and we suggest that you give thought as to how to change your organization's culture. Working on expanding your employees' comfort zones will be an essential first step on the road to making your organization a place where this talent pool can thrive.

Conclusion and the way forward

Chapter 7 reviewed how employees are onboarded, emphasizing that how neurodiverse employees are treated early with a new employer can shape their impressions of the people and the corporate culture in which they find themselves. The next chapter focuses on training and developing neurodiverse employees.

Web-based resources for this chapter

- http://jvschicago.org/successfully-bring-new-hires-on-board/
- http://hrdailyadvisor.blr.com/2014/03/31/how-to-make-internal-hiring-support-more-disabled-friendly/

A Tool for Reflecting on How to Make Onboarding More Sensitive to Neurodiverse People

Directions: Use this tool to guide your thinking, and that of others in your organization, on how to change the employee onboarding process so that new hires from the neurodiverse community can seamlessly transition into the organization as a whole and their new positions. For each question appearing in the left column below, write your answers in the right column. Then compare your thoughts to others in the organization – including the thoughts of people with neurologically based disabilities. While there are no right or wrong answers to the questions, the goal of this tool is to increase the likelihood that the organization's onboarding process will result in newly hired members of the neurodiverse community seamlessly transitioning into the organization and their roles.

	Questions	Your Answers
1	How are employees typically onboarded into your organization? Describe the process step by step.	
2	How should employees be onboarded in your organization to enable newly hired neurodiverse employees to achieve self-efficacy as quickly as possible?	
3	What laws, rules, or regulations might affect the employee onboarding process in your jurisdiction as regards people with neurologically based disabilities?	
4	What do co-workers and managers need to do differently during the onboarding process to enable newly hired neurodiverse employees to achieve self-efficacy as quickly as possible?	

What to do after reading this chapter

1. Meet with some of your key HR staff to discuss the four levels of onboarding from a neurodiversity perspective.
2. Think about the pushback you might get from key decision-makers when it comes to integrating people from the neurodiverse community into your organization.
3. Revisit your feedback tools from a neurodiversity perspective.
4. Establish a task force like The ABC Company did.
5. Identify your organization's critical vulnerabilities when it comes to integrating people from the neurodiverse community into your organization. What are your weak spots?

8 Training and development for neurodiversity

The next day, Victoria and Harriet met to discuss how to proceed after their meeting with The ABC Company's key decision-makers. Victoria said, "For now, I'd like to start by brainstorming with you about how we might rethink our training and development from a neurodiversity perspective. That way, when the task force is formed, we will have thought through the issues as they relate to training and development."

Scope of training

Harriet looked thoughtful. "I agree. As I remember from my graduate studies, 'training involved four phases: assessing needs; designing programs; implementing and delivering the training; and evaluating program results.' I think that, if we reflect upon those four phases for neurodiverse employees, we'll surface what needs our attention and get an initial idea how to deal with them" (Belcourt, Singh, Bohlander & Snell, 2014. Pg. 238).

Phase one: conducting the needs assessment

Victoria opened to a page of a document on her computer. "About 30 percent of larger firms – including GE, Walmart, and IBM – have what are called chief learning officers. These people are top executives within their firms who are responsible for making certain that a company's training is timely and focused on the firm's top strategic issues (Belcourt, Singh, Bohlander & Snell, 2014. Pg. 239). On the one hand, we're in good shape because, as you saw from the meeting, the decision-makers recognize the importance of integrating people with disabilities into the firm. I expect that this issue will get more attention and will be regarded as a top strategic issue once the task force gets off the ground. That said, we do not have a chief learning officer. In the absence of one, which has a substantial cost, it is up to me to ensure that training is focused on issues like this. I have to tell you, if we had a Chief Learning Officer (CLO), I'd be happy to hand this off to her because there is so much I don't know when it comes to aligning training to organizational strategic goals."

DOI: 10.4324/9781351207478-8

Harriet took a sip of her juice. "Perhaps we ought to advocate for creating a CLO position?"

"I've been thinking the same thing. You know, creating another C-level position is not just a cost issue because when you do so, you also put someone else around the boardroom table. So, I wanted to give them time to digest this issue before I raised the possibility of bringing a CLO on board. However, I agree with you. I think that creating the position of CLO is going to be critical to our ability to provide training and development that is suited to the needs of individual employees with disabilities and that is aligned with the strategic needs of the company."

Organization analysis

"Right off the cuff, I can foresee two issues that we're going to have to rethink," Victoria said, referring to a relevant section of HR reading she had on her laptop. "First, we're going to have to rethink how we collect data. We both know that 'HR practitioners often gather information on the organization's labor costs and related information on turnover, absenteeism, and health and safety' (Belcourt, Singh, Bohlander & Snell, 2014. Pg. 241). Well, that's what HR folks usually do. However, once we're looking at doing an organizational analysis to see how to integrate neurodiverse employees into the form, then we will likely have to deal with sensitive personal information that is different in nature and scope."

"You mean things like assessments from subject matter experts and clinicians like psychologists, psychiatrists, learning experts, and the like?"

"Yes, that's what I am referring to," said Victoria. "The process of collecting information to conduct an organizational analysis is likely going to entail collecting information related to people's disabilities. HR folks are going to be engaged in dealing with information that is more personal and more sensitive than they are accustomed to and to doing so on a more frequent basis than in the past. As you said, we're going to be dealing with confidential and sensitive information from specialists. We're going to have to think about how to deal with that, especially in light of employee privacy laws. Who's going to collect this information? Where's it going to be stored? Onsite? Offsite? Will we collect it? Will we have to hire an outside third party to do it?"

"I'm starting to appreciate the ramifications for data collection when it comes to conducting an organizational analysis," Harriet said.

"The second issue relates to what we said in the meeting," said Victoria. "Gone are the days of purchasing 'off-the-shelf' course materials developed by external training companies. I think we will have to make a shift to individualized training that's been developed in-house. I don't have all the details of how that must work, but I think that's the general direction we must head."

"It looks like we're not just talking about hiring a CLO but also talking about hiring people to develop individualized training programs and course materials in-house."

88 *Training and development for neurodiversity*

Victoria said, "I think that, if we want to do this right, we may have to invest in having more assets available in-house. That is a question of values – what we care about – and the willingness of our senior leaders to act on those values. Remember, we've already established that one principle of successfully working to integrate people with disabilities is the willingness to course-correct continuously until the organization finds the best path. If we develop course materials and training programs in-house, it makes it much easier to course-correct as needed."

Task analysis

"I can envisage two challenges when it comes to conducting a task analysis for disabled employees," said Harriet as she referred to some HR reading material on her laptop. " 'The first step in task analysis is to list all tasks or duties included in the job' (Belcourt, Singh, Bohlander & Snell, 2014. Pg. 241). Well, we've established that the tasks or duties may well be up for negotiation. So it seems clear that we can't do a task analysis until we've had the input from a multi-disciplinary team. Second, the next step in task analysis is to take and compile an inventory of the steps performed by a worker to carry out each task (Belcourt, Singh, Bohlander & Snell, 2014). Evidently, these steps are going to vary on an individual basis. Third, we know that the general trend these days is to use teams and that teams require more flexibility than when individuals perform all tasks (Belcourt, Singh, Bohlander & Snell, 2014). So, it looks like another challenge is how to integrate disabled employees into teams. That seems to be a two-way challenge. The teams need to be willing to incorporate disabled employees, and disabled employees should learn how to be flexible."

Person analysis

Victoria glanced at the reading material on Harriet's laptop. "You know, like many companies, we have summarized performance management information as a personal analysis. That means we summarize everything we know about each worker in one form so that we have access to critical information in one place. In most cases, a performance appraisal might indicate that an employee is not meeting performance requirements but usually does not reveal causes" (Belcourt, Singh, Bohlander & Snell, 2014).

"I know what you mean. I always found that to be a pretty frustrating aspect of conducting performance appraisals. They reveal the gap, but not why the gap exists."

"So we can see that, if performance appraisals don't tell us why gaps in expectations exist for the general population, then that will certainly be the case for disabled employees," said Victoria. "The general approach that I've followed throughout my career, and I believe the one we follow here, is that company managers should talk to employees so they can agree on what to do."

"I think our managers will need special training to have these conversations with disabled employees," said Harriet. "At the same time, the research I did with the people I met showed me that, if disabled employees perceive their managers to be sincerely offering them opportunities for improvement, they will likely embrace the chance to determine development approaches that are beneficial to the individual and the organization. I want to emphasize that, based on the research I've done, it seems that the success of manager-employee dialogs depends on employees feeling comfortable having disability-related dialogs with their managers. If they don't feel comfortable, then it is highly unlikely that managers will get the information they need."

Phase two: designing the training program

"Evidently we will have to invest in appropriate training to ensure that managers know how to have these dialogs," said Victoria. "We've acknowledged our efforts to integrate people with disabilities will take place within our organizational culture. Just as we speak of an organizational environment, so too we can speak of a learning environment. So, notwithstanding the challenges we've just discussed, I think we need to think through the learning environment necessary to enhance learning for disabled employees. From a brief professional development course I took some time ago I remember that four important issues are the training objectives, the motivation of learners, the principles of learning, and instructor characteristics (Belcourt, Singh, Bohlander & Snell, 2014). Can you share your perspective with me based on your various meetings, site visits, and research?"

Training objectives

"When it comes to training objectives, I think we're going to have to distinguish between the substantive objective and the time frame," said Harriet. "When it comes to a person with a learning disability, we must ask two questions. First, is the knowledge or skill to be acquired appropriate for learners with their learning profile? Second, what might be an appropriate time frame? The reality is that we might not know what an appropriate or realistic time frame is until the neurodiverse employee has tried out the task. However, I do know from my research that it can be stressful for people with learning disabilities to master a task when they need more time than others. The need for more time results in having to request accommodations in the form of time-flexibility, and this can be stressful because many employers are not sympathetic to such requests. So, what I'm saying is that once we determine whether a skill is appropriate for an employee with a disability, then we should be open to suspending a time frame until the employee has tried it out so we can jointly determine a realistic time frame."

"So we're back to the theme of suspending and modifying expectations?"

"Correct. Suspending and modifying expectations is key."

"What have you learned about the role of learner motivation?"

90 *Training and development for neurodiversity*

Learner readiness and motivation

Harriet gestured to Victoria to look at the HR reading she had on her laptop. "The good news is that our organization is already grouping individuals according to their ability to learn based on tests, assessment information, or other methods (Belcourt, Singh, Bohlander & Snell, 2014). Then we provide alternative instruction when needed. If it is accepted practice for the general population, then it is all the more so for people with disabilities."

"Did you notice any difference in readiness and motivation among the people with disabilities you met in the course of your research?"

"Funny you should say that," said Harriet. "I found the people I met who have disabilities seemed to be highly motivated. In fact, at this point, it is clear to me that many disabled candidates might be even more motivated than candidates from the general population."

"That's interesting. How do you explain that?"

"Well, it comes down to perseverance and resilience. Take for example recent college graduates with a disability. By the time they get to us, they have had to overcome multiple challenges. They might not have been expected to get into university in the first place. Once they do, they have had to overcome many challenges within the university to get their degree. When they're finished with their degree, they've had to look for an employer who will not just give them a break after they graduate but do so in a manner that accommodates their disability. So, my research and experience show me that disabled employees we've got sitting in our training program are highly motivated to succeed."

"Well, that's great," said Victoria. "Then I guess we're in great shape."

"Yes, the fact that disabled employees are highly motivated is good news. However, even the most highly motivated new hire can become demotivated in an unsupportive organizational culture. The new hire can have all the motivation in the world, but if the other things we've discussed are not in place, then we should not be surprised if they grow frustrated."

"Point taken," said Victoria. "I see that. I'm glad to hear that disabled new hires are highly motivated. That will be a great point to mention when we have follow-up conversations with people like Fred, who have their doubts about this. Now, I remember from that professional development course I took that training must help workers transition from outside to meeting a unique organization's requirements. How might the principles of learning be applied to disabled employees? What principles of learning must be applied to disabled employees?"

Principles of learning

"The principles cover the 'importance of setting learning goals, making the presentation meaningful to learners, demonstrating the learning, accounting for individual differences, giving opportunities for practice, using whole-versus-part learning, and providing feedback on the learning,'" said Harriet (Belcourt, Singh, Bohlander & Snell, 2014. Pg. 245).

"Correct," said Victoria.

"It is not possible to say with certainty what the implications are for all people with all disabilities in all industries at all times," said Harriet. "That said, two points come to mind immediately. First, it is already established that, when it comes to the general population, variety is essential because people differ in learning styles. If that is true for the general population, then it is indeed so for learning-disabled employees, for example. Trainers understand the need to accommodate different learning styles (Belcourt, Singh, Bohlander & Snell, 2014). What will have to be determined are the details as they relate to specific employees and their unique needs.

"The second point is on feedback and reinforcement. We know that 'learners provide some feedback by monitoring themselves, while other feedback comes from trainers and other learners' (Belcourt, Singh, Bohlander & Snell, 2014. Pg. 245). Several issues come to mind here. The first is that it might be challenging for some people with neurologically based disabilities to provide feedback about themselves by self-monitoring if they face challenges about self-awareness. The second is that trainers and fellow trainees must know of, and be sensitive to, the disability-related needs of a disabled colleague."

Victoria said, "Would I be correct in saying that the overall approach to these principles is going to be one of individualization on a case-by-case basis?"

"That is correct. Ultimately, we need to bring in the multi-disciplinary teams we've discussed. Once the team has had the opportunity to work with an employee, only then will it be possible to determine how each principle applies to one employee in one role."

"You know, I'd love to hear about any insights you gleaned from your research when it comes to the difference between training methods for non-managerial versus managerial employees," said Victoria. "However, in the interests of time, we will have to wrap up this conversation. Harriet, I would be interested in seeing a written overview of all that we've discussed. I'm especially interested in the effectiveness of the human resources manual from the perspective of people with disabilities. When do you think you could prepare something like that for me?"

Phase three: implementing the training program

Training methods for non-managerial employees

Since Victoria and Harriet have wrapped up their conversation, let's leave The ABC Company and summarize issues for the rest of the chapter.

Though on-the-job-training (OJT) is a method that is often used, it's important to know that it has its imperfections. For example, what if a manager doesn't have the familiarity of how to do OJT? What if a new hire isn't thoroughly informed of their specific tasks? Two methods can be used to mitigate these problems: have specific training goals and have time slots set aside during training to engage in feedback or

92 *Training and development for neurodiversity*

evaluation (Belcourt, Singh, Bohlander & Snell, 2014). It is essential that trainers assist managers in ensuring the office environment is as learning-friendly as possible. Additionally, it is beneficial for managers to support new hires in gauging their job successes and endeavor to help them improve (Belcourt, Singh, Bohlander & Snell, 2014. Pg. 249).

Here are a few ways you might consider the points we've raised from a disability perspective:

1 A well-structured training environment is imperative. That means that the who, what, where, and when of training must all be structured toward the needs of disabled employees.
2 If poor training skills by managers is a problem for the general population, then it will be even more so for training employees with disabilities. You may wish to consider sensitivity training for your managers. A manager must be sensitive to, and familiar with, such issues as the suitability of training content, mode of training delivery, establishing a training environment, the role of assistive technology, and others.
3 The absence of well-defined job performance criteria is an acknowledged problem in the general population. Perhaps trainers should try to be flexible with job performance criteria.
4 Consider course-correcting with a team-based approach to job performance criteria.
5 When it comes to developing realistic goals as suggested by training experts, we think that it's important to be comfortable with taking a trial-and-error approach.
6 We agree with the suggestion made by training experts to plan a schedule for each trainee with the proviso it is not rigid and that all stakeholders understand that the schedule may be revised as needed.
7 Not only should an environment be established that is non-threatening and conducive to training, but it should also be supportive. All aspects of training – the who, what, where, and why – all need to be aligned with the unique needs of a particular disabled employee.

Internships

There are some standard textbook suggestions on how to conduct successful internships. For example: making sure that the intern has the right amount of training for the expected tasks, eliciting ideas for intern tasks from fellow employees, and bringing in a mentor so the intern can be guided and supervised (Belcourt, Singh, Bohlander & Snell, 2014). It is also advisable to have the interns positioned around and exposed to different parts of the office, as well as offering them the opportunity to sit in on meetings. It is advantageous to think long term with interns as well, by mapping out procedures that enable interns to eventually be hired (Belcourt, Singh, Bohlander & Snell, 2014. Pg. 251).

Training and development for neurodiversity 93

Viewing internships for the neurodiverse community, we would recommend the following considerations.

1 Review accomplishable tasks for clarity and detail. Take care to make sure that the project assigned is accomplishable and be very thorough. Engage more stakeholders than would be necessary for an intern with no disability.
2 Consider whether suitable employees who do not have disabilities can mentor interns with disabilities and, if so, what training might be needed to give an employee who serves as a mentor.
3 Solicit project suggestions from other staff members if you are comfortable with the possibility of receiving recommendations that are not suitable for interns with disabilities.

Some organizations rotate interns throughout their organization and invite them to staff meetings. However, for interns with disabilities, we suggest that you consider the vulnerabilities of the organization regarding the current culture. Rotating interns with disabilities throughout the organization and treating them as part of the organizational staff can only happen once the right organizational culture has been established. So, we assess that organizations should think about holding off on implementing an internship program for disabled students until it has the organizational culture to support it and the accompanying supportive infrastructure.

Re-thinking classroom instruction and online instruction for neurodiverse employees can help to surface two critical issues to consider when you think about training employees with disabilities.

Classroom instruction

When most people think of training, they think of classroom instruction. Most organizational training still occurs in classrooms (Belcourt, Singh, Bohlander & Snell, 2014). For classroom instruction, two issues must be addressed. The first is the technical issue relating to how classroom instruction must be adapted to meet the needs of disabled employees. That's a matter of making the right adaptations and modifications that we know can be made one way or the other by consulting subject experts and by asking employees with neurologically based disabilities.

However, we want to surface another issue. When classroom instruction happens, then modifications, adaptations, and accommodations occur in public. How can individual and group needs be balanced? If someone with a neurologically based disability wants to record a meeting, and other people do not feel comfortable with that, what should happen? How can organizational leaders balance the needs of a disabled employee with the concerns of people who might not feel comfortable with having the meeting being recorded?

94 *Training and development for neurodiversity*

Online instruction

Increasingly, companies are utilizing online resources for instruction, which has the benefit of workers conveniently learning at their stations when not involved in other work projects (Belcourt, Singh, Bohlander & Snell, 2014).

But online instruction has its drawbacks for neurodiverse employees. One is that employees who are learning at their desks online may be subjected to drop-by visitors, momentary phone calls, and other distractions. While that can be troublesome for neurotypical employees, it is all the more so for neurodiverse workers who may not be readily able to switch from one task to another.

What is needed is flexibility. It is vital to ask neurodiverse employees what accommodations they might need to ensure that they can learn effectively. Then organizational leaders must be willing to make those accommodations.

Phase four: evaluating the training program

We want to help you think about how evaluating training might differ for neurodiverse employees.

Make sure that employees with disabilities have clear learning goals as they begin participation in a training program. Remember that disappointment is a function of expectations. It is a well-known fact that little off-the-job training transfers back to a job in changed behavior. So, if this is a problem for the general population, then it is more so for people with disabilities. We suggest that we pay particular attention to two approaches.

1 "Ensure that the training environment resembles the job environment. Job transfer, which means taking what is learned in training and applying it back on the job, works best when the features of the training setting are close to those of the work setting" (Belcourt, Singh, Bohlander & Snell, 2014. Pg. 259).
2 Give employees transfer strategies. "Employees are most likely to transfer back to the job what they learned in training when they are guided to plan for transfer while still in training" (Belcourt, Singh, Bohlander & Snell, 2014. Pg. 261). The same principle applies to disabled workers. Make sure that they have a plan by the end of training so that they know how to apply back to their jobs what they learned in training and have been guided to consider, and plan for, overcoming any obstacles they can think of for on-the-job application of training.

Addressing the question of return on investment (ROI) of training for employees from the neurodiverse community is tricky because when managers and executives ask about ROI, they often want to see short-term results. It is widely understood in the training world that some benefits may take long time periods to appear and to be realized. We are not saying it is impossible to measure ROI. But we are saying that the starting point must be an understanding that measuring ROI for training is an issue not just for employees with disabilities. Employees with disabilities have lower turnover rates but may take longer to demonstrate benefits of training.

Team training and cross-training

Many workplaces are moving, or have moved, to team-based work. Much work is performed on project teams with many people. Individual contributions may be difficult to identify (Belcourt, Singh, Bohlander & Snell, 2014). But teams must be trained on how to work with people with disabilities. Just as the organizational culture must be supportive of people with disabilities, the team climate must also be favorable.

The same issue should also be addressed for cross-training. When teams perform work that depends on many people, then all employees should be trained to cover for others who may be absent. That requires cross-training so that individuals can step in and do the work of others (Belcourt, Singh, Bohlander & Snell, 2014).

For disabled employees, two points are relevant here. On the one hand, there are employees with learning disabilities who may wish to be cross-trained but are having a sufficiently difficult time with one job, never mind able to perform multiple jobs. There are other employees with autism who prefer very focused positions that might seem monotonous to the general population but which are well-suited to them.

We invite you to think about the leadership roles that might be needed to facilitate the integration of people with disabilities. Do you have someone in your organization who can take responsibility for making the training and development of disabled employees a priority? Are you willing to consider the possibility of more individualized training?

Take this opportunity to think about your organization's culture again. What might the implications be for team training and cross-training for neurodiverse employees? Finally, how well attuned is your organization to the ethical issues you will likely have to address? If you or your organization are unwilling to create the leadership role described above, then please consider why not. What are the constraints? If you are not attuned to the ethical issues related above, then we suggest that now would be a good time to appraise yourself and seek expert counsel where possible.

Conclusion and the way forward

Chapter 8 focused on training and developing neurodiverse employees. The next chapter examines how to rethink performance management to encourage people who have neurologically based disabilities.

Web-based resources for this chapter

- www.hrtips.org/list_1.cfm?c_id=61&view_all=true

96 *Training and development for neurodiversity*

A Tool for Reflecting on How to Make Training and Development More Sensitive to Neurodiverse Employees	
Directions: Use this tool to guide your thinking, and that of others in your organization, on how to make the employee training and development process more likely to lead to the successful integration of people with neurologically based disabilities. For each question appearing in the left column below, write your answers in the right column. Then compare your thoughts to others in the organization – including the thoughts of people with neurologically based disabilities. While there are no right or wrong answers to the questions, the goal of this tool is to reflect on how the organization's traditional process of training and development can be changed to increase the likelihood of successfully integrating people with neurologically based disabilities.	
Questions	**Your Answers**
1 How are employees typically trained and developed in your organization? Describe the process step by step.	
2 How should employees be trained and developed in your organization to increase the likelihood of successfully integrating people with neurologically based disabilities?	
3 What laws, rules, or regulations might affect the employee training and development process in your jurisdiction regarding neurodiverse employees?	
4 How can workers and managers conduct themselves differently during the training and development process to increase the likelihood of successfully integrating people with neurologically based disabilities into your organization?	

What to do after reading this chapter

1 Investigate the possibility of creating a chief learning officer in your organization.
2 Identify the line managers who might need sensitivity training before they're ready to work with neurodiverse employees.
3 Ask some of your staff how they feel about the possibility of being recorded during meetings.
4 Establish quiet zones where neurodiverse employees can get online training with minimal or no interruptions.
5 Examine your budget. Do you have the resources necessary to develop course materials and training programs in-house?

9 Performance management for neurodiversity

How should performance feedback and performance management be handled differently for people with disabilities? This chapter will address that question.

A traditional approach to HR regards performance feedback as a straightforward issue. During a session to discuss performance with workers, managers and HR professionals should outline what is expected or appropriate behaviors, ensure that when feedback is given it is directed to the behavior rather than to the individual, and offer feedback constructively. Feedback, moreover, ought to be provided in an expeditious fashion, in a manner in which it is not too much information to handle, and cognizant of what the employee can manage. During the feedback sessions, it is equally important to make sure that the employee understands what is being said, and knows what their next steps are (Belcourt, Singh, Bohlander & Snell, 2014. Pg. 283).

So, let's start with item one on the list. From our perspective, we think that some "undesirable behaviors" could be attributed to the manner in which some people experience neurological conditions (Belcourt, Singh, Bohlander & Snell, 2014). Think for a moment about people with obsessive-compulsive disorder (OCD). That condition might lead them to check their work more often than the rest of the population. HR professionals should make sure that disabled employees are not unnecessarily criticized for such behavior.

Second, focusing feedback on the behavior and not on the person is critical (Belcourt, Singh, Bohlander & Snell, 2014). Many people with disabilities are not self-aware. However, just as workers should be sensitized to how they should behave when co-workers disclose their disabilities, so too should disabled workers' behaviors be pointed out to them when how they behave affects their job performance.

Third, "frame feedback to help the employee succeed" (Belcourt, Singh, Bohlander & Snell, 2014. Pg. 283). We think that, from a disability perspective, the manager-employee relationship is essential here. It is vital that managers establish trusting relationships with all employees. After all, that feedback is not given in a vacuum; rather, it is offered in a pre-existing relationship. If managers have shown themselves to be sensitive to neurodiversity-related issues, workers will be more willing to listen and act on manager recommendations. Conversely, if the

DOI: 10.4324/9781351207478-9

Performance appraisal programs might not succeed in their objectives, for several
Performance management for neurodiversity 99

manager has a track record of not delivering on disability-related requests, then that diminishes trust and makes it more difficult for employees to believe their managers want them to succeed.

Fourth, "direct the feedback to behavior the employee can control" (Belcourt, Singh, Bohlander & Snell, 2014. Pg. 283). That is a sensitive matter for people with neurologically based conditions. It is crucial for managers and employers to have open conversations with employees who have neurologically based disabilities so that everyone understands the effects of these conditions. If an employee has a learning disability, for example, then criticizing them for not catching onto concepts as quickly as their colleagues is inappropriate.

The fifth and sixth points are that the "feedback should be timely and that feedback should be limited to what the employee can process" (Belcourt, Singh, Bohlander & Snell, 2014. Pg. 283). These principles apply as much to people with neurologically based disabilities as for anyone else. However, from a developmental perspective, performance management should open a dialog between a manager and a worker about how the worker's goals align with those of the organization. Here is a pivotal point to understand about many people with non-visible disabilities. The gap between their strengths and weaknesses is often more significant than the difference between the strengths and weaknesses of people the general population. So, we should be willing to course-correct periodically (and perhaps more than we would be willing to do for the general population) to make sure that neurodiverse employees play to their strengths. By doing that, the manager can achieve two results. First, it gives employees the satisfaction of working in ways consistent with their strengths and avoids the stress that results from their weaknesses. Second, by doing that, the employer minimizes the need for accommodations.

With that as background, let's turn back to Harriet and Victoria in The ABC Company.

"Based on my research," Harriet began, "perhaps the greatest single thing that employers can do is to find a way to align disabled employees with work that matches their strengths."

"Isn't that asking us to change roles?" asked Victoria. "From being HR professionals to career counselors?"

"You're right, it does, to a certain extent. Here's the key point. We're going to have to step out of the box, out of our comfort zones, and be willing to wear different hats. Now, we've established that we have to be willing to suspend setting goals until we have been able to clarify expectations. How do you discuss goals when the goals are in flux?"

Why appraisals programs sometimes fail

Performance appraisal programs might not succeed in their objectives, for several main reasons: when there is little face-to-face contact between a superior and those being appraised, if a manager believes it's not worth the time or energy spent, when there are marked differences between a job description and the appraisal form, if

100 *Performance management for neurodiversity*

follow-up is lacking, or when the appraisal is centered on mistakes rather than successes (Belcourt, Singh, Bohlander & Snell, 2014. Pg. 285).

> Managers might also feel unprepared to accommodate special requests from disabled employees, might feel discomfort in what they perceive to be a judgmental or confrontational in-person appraisal situation, or they do not know how to evaluate performance.
>
> (Belcourt, Singh, Bohlander & Snell, 2014. Pg. 285)

The following are our concerns from a neurodiversity perspective:

1 Managers must feel that the investment of time and energy is worthwhile. There is a risk that managers might get worn out by having to invest time and energy in appraisals for people with disabilities because they take more time and effort than for others.
2 Managers may feel they have to deal with more issues than with other employees.
3 There is a judgmental role for appraisals. Managers must put this aside and adopt a helping role. Have your managers achieved the right balance between judging and helping? If they have not, HR should give them training to help them improve that balance.
4 We are concerned about an appraisal being a once-a-year event. People with disabilities need constant and ongoing feedback. Having an appraisal as an annual event risks letting issues accumulate and fester. While it may be a good idea for a compensation review to take place annually, we suggest that performance appraisals ought to take place on a quarterly basis with the possibility of allowing for monthly check-ins. Having appraisals on a quarterly basis can be a win-win situation for both employee and manager. For an employee, it means there are no surprises. Eliminating the element of surprise may also help to reduce anxiety. It will only have been three months since the last appraisal, so there is no need to be concerned that a mountain of issues has accumulated. We now return to see how Victoria and Harriet are coming along.

Developing an effective appraisal program

"So Harriet, how should we go about developing an effective appraisal program from a disability perspective?"

"Well," Harriet said, "according to conventional HR theory, 'performance standards should be established and communicated to workers before they are measured against those standards. Job standards should be based on the work activities and duties listed on job descriptions' (Belcourt, Singh, Bohlander & Snell, 2014. Pg. 287). I think we need to rank the priorities in job requirements. I suggest we consider some staggered appraisals. Let's say that there are three categories of requirements, then we would have three appraisals staggered sequentially. First, appraise the most critical requirements. Then have the employee take on the second-most important job requirements and appraise those. Finally, have the

Performance management for neurodiversity 101

employee take on the third-most essential requirements followed by an appraisal" (Belcourt, Singh, Bohlander & Snell, 2014. Pg. 287).

"Good! The next issue would be the matter of strategic relevance."

Strategic relevance

"Correct," Harriet said. " 'Strategic relevance means that workers are held account-able for helping the organization achieve its strategic goals' (Belcourt, Singh, Bohlander & Snell, 2014. Pg. 288). There should be some logical relationship between what a worker does and organizational requirements. For example, if an organization has established a standard that '95 percent of all customer complaints are to be resolved in one day' (Belcourt, Singh, Bohlander & Snell, 2014. Pg. 288), then it is relevant for the customer service representatives to be held to this standard when evaluated."

Victoria said, "This raises the issue of what to do when there is a discrepancy between organizational standards and the performance of disabled employees. What should we do if 95 percent of all customer complaints are to be resolved in a day, but a disabled employee can only resolve 80 percent of the complaints in a day? Do we give them more time, or do we lower company standards? Do we lower the standards for that employee?"

"No," said Harriet. "The solution is going to depend on individuals, their roles, and other factors. That said, I don't think the right approach is to lower company standards. The answer rests in working with a neurodiverse employee to close the gap. We should still keep the standard at 95 percent but work with disabled employees to come up with plans to close the gap. In the interim, I would suggest that some of the load be assigned to the neurodiverse employee's co-workers. Perhaps some of the co-workers' work, which disabled employees can perform, should also be transferred to them at the same time."

"I can foresee resistance when some employees are asked to pick up some of the slack."

"I can, too," said Harriet. "But that's why organizational culture is so important. Examples like this dramatize the importance of educating our employees as to why this is important. As things currently stand, I think that many employees might take a short-term view and think that what we are asking them to do is unfair. However, I believe that an organization-wide educational initiative can help people understand that, by temporarily picking up slack, they will not only help individuals adjust to company standards but will also help the company achieve necessary results over the longer term because there is a greater prospect that we will be able to keep that employee if we can bring that person up to company standards."

"In reading HR literature on performance management, I see another issue to consider is 'criterion deficiency' (Belcourt, Singh, Bohlander & Snell, 2014). The concept is simple enough. 'It means that performance standards should capture the full range of employee responsibilities. When one criterion is given undue prominence – such as sales revenues for a salesperson – but other criteria are ignored,

102 *Performance management for neurodiversity*

then the performance standards suffer from criterion deficiency' (Belcourt, Singh, Bohlander & Snell, 2014. Pg. 288). What are the implications from a disability perspective?"

"Interesting you ask that question," said Harriet. "This issue makes me think about how we might take a more holistic approach to appraising people with disabilities as they progress through the different levels of job function. I think we should expand the evaluation criteria so that, even though disabled employees may struggle with the first layer of job requirements, they are acknowledged for having a constructive attitude in their work and their level of motivation. If the scope of performance recognition is regarded more broadly, we will help them to persist and master more job-related requirements."

"We have always been quite persistent about the issue of reliability," said Victoria. "I printed out the handout you emailed me. To paraphrase, reliability means how much workers sustain performance levels over time."

"I am pleased you raise this issue for two reasons. First, this is an example of how standards are going to be different for disabled employees. Typically, we expect consistent performance from our employees. However, we need to understand that performance may fluctuate over time for disabled employees rather than have them maintain consistent performance levels. Reliability also helps to re-surface expectations. We have acknowledged that we may have to modify our expectations."

"It is not just us who will have to modify expectations, but when I think about who has input into our appraisal process, there is a wide range of parties who contribute. At The ABC Company, we gather input from many stakeholders: managers, supervisors, the individual employee, peers, team members, customers, and sometimes subordinates. How might getting appraisals from all those people change when it comes to getting feedback from an employee with a neurologically based disability?"

"Let's start with managers and supervisors," said Harriet. "Receiving appraisals from so many people presents an opportunity and a challenge for employees with neurologically based disabilities. On the one hand, it is an opportunity because we can get information from many people. That should give us a richer, more holistic picture than if we had feedback from just a manager. On the other hand, that we receive appraisals from so many people begs the question as to whether we should inform some or all of them about the person's disability. Clearly, we would need a disabled employee's permission for that."

"Right, the problem is that if we do not inform them of the existence of a disability, how valuable is their feedback? We could essentially be faced with the frustrating situation of having much invalid data."

"Correct. So, for managers, looking at the material I've gathered from the web, I note that managers frequently complain that they have insufficient time to observe employee performance. Frankly, this is one of our vulnerabilities. Our managers are just so short of time that even if we go through sensitizing them to what they should pay attention to, I am concerned that many would not have the time to do that. Not out of malice, just because of a lack of time."

Performance management for neurodiversity   103

"So it looks like one of the critical success factors here is to make sure that we assign disabled employees to managers who have the time and willingness to pay attention to their special needs."

"Correct," said Harriet. "We can have all the sensitivity training and organization-wide initiatives we want, but if the manager assigned to a disabled employee is stretched beyond limits, then the needs of the neurodiverse employee will not even be a blip on the manager's radar screen. Now I'd like to comment on self-appraisals. I think that the advantages of self-appraisals might be of mixed value for disabled workers. Many people with disabilities have a keen level of self-awareness, so they know what they are good at doing and what they are not good at doing. On the other hand, many people with neurologically based disabilities may have a diminished sense of social awareness and hence may be less attuned to the behavioral and interpersonal issues that factor into a self-appraisal. The result is that the discrepancy between a neurodiverse employee's self-appraisal and how they're perceived by others might be greater than the discrepancy between a neurotypical employee's self-appraisal and how they are perceived by others."

"I would think that subordinate appraisals are less pertinent for the time being since disabled employees are likely to come in at junior positions. However, we will eventually need to rethink how we approach peer, team, and customer appraisals."

"I agree, for now, subordinate appraisals are likely to be less pertinent. That said, I'd like to refer to what I found about peer appraisals. Peer appraisal is valuable because peers frequently see performance dimensions that supervisors miss. 'Current thinking suggests that peers do better than supervisors on noticing leadership skills and interpersonal skills' (Belcourt, Singh, Bohlander & Snell, 2014. Pg. 292). While that might be true for the general population, I see some issues for disabled employees. It is precisely about performance dimensions that I am concerned. I believe it is critical for peers to be aware of a colleague's disability. Otherwise, they will not know how to make sense of behavior stemming from neurologically based differences, and we risk receiving feedback that is unhelpful and even hurtful. Imagine appraisal comments that say, 'he never looks at me in the face when we're speaking,' or 'she keeps on checking her work,' or 'she persistently shows up late.' If people making those comments were aware that their colleagues have Asperger's syndrome or that they were checking their work and or showing up late due to OCD, then those comments would be less likely to appear on appraisals."

"So, it looks like we are going to have to navigate carefully who employees disclose to and how much they disclose?"

"Exactly," said Harriet. "Although keep in mind that disclosure is not an all or nothing matter. That said, you are correct. Disclosure is also pertinent to team appraisals. Organizations have developed team appraisals to evaluate the performance of their teams as a whole. A few issues come to mind when we think about integrating disabled employees into teams. Can they match the team standards, or does the team have to adjust to the capabilities of the neurodiverse

104 *Performance management for neurodiversity*

employee? What are the benchmarks against which the neurodiverse employee and the team are evaluated? Also, when it comes to accommodations, we have already referred to the potential conflict between individual needs and group comfort levels. That might occur when a disabled employee needs to record a meeting and others around the table are not comfortable with having themselves recorded."

"These are good questions, but I have to admit that they are questions that I have never faced before. This is new territory for me. I've never thought about it, and how to calibrate team performance standards to accommodate a disabled team member, so I am a little bit out of my depth here. My first thought is that we should try to have disabled employees work themselves up to team standards over time, but I admit that's not an evidence-based decision. I'm not sure what research there is out there either for adjusting team standards to accommodate disabled employees or for how to get a disabled employee to match team standards. Now, what do we do about customer appraisals? I have to tell you that's what I am anxious about. So far we have been discussing the dynamics of managing this issue for internal stakeholders. If we have not worked it out internally, how are we going to address this matter for external stakeholders?"

"I share your concerns," said Harriet. "There is much at stake when it comes to external stakeholders like external customers. Not only the dollar value of the business that a given customer does with us but also the impact on our brand. If we get this right, there is much to be gained regarding increased customer loyalty, referrals, community image, and goodwill in the marketplace. On the other hand, as the expression goes, 'it takes years to build a reputation and five minutes to destroy it.' So, the root issue is whether a specific person is suited to a customer-facing role altogether. If he or she is suitable, we might get into what you referred to as the touchy territory of the disclosure. Depending on the individual employee and the customer, it might be feasible to have a four-way consult with someone from HR, the neurodiverse employee, their manager, and the customer to think through how to bring together all four stakeholders. I think that, if we can have a meeting of the minds, then customer appraisal will reflect that context. However, I would be concerned about a customer appraisal without this context."

"I think that's a good starting point. But there is much to do, and we would need to look at this issue on a case-by-case basis. You know, with my background in psychology, one issue that comes to mind is how we are going to address biases and errors when it comes to appraisers."

Training appraisers

"I share that concern, and I can relate to it personally," said Harriet. "I am concerned about two issues. 'First is the halo error; second is the horn error. The halo error means that a manager or rater forms an unshakeable positive impression of a worker; the horn error is the opposite'" (Belcourt, Singh, Bohlander & Snell, 2014. Pg. 298). I am concerned about the horn error. The challenge is that,

Performance management for neurodiversity 105

on the one hand, managers like to get things off their 'to do list.' On the other hand, when working with and accommodating a person with a disability, requests for disability-related accommodations might stay on their to-do list for a long time because the nature and extent of disability accommodations may change over time. Frankly, the risk is that, for even the most patient managers, they might perceive an employee as 'Mr. or Ms. Can-You-Please-Accommodate-Me', and they might resent that person. Without us doing the right advance groundwork and without the right systems in place, at a certain point we might face managers asking, 'Harriet, when is this going to be off my plate?' So, I raise this point here because I'm concerned that, if the scenario I have just described plays itself out, then the horn error could be one of those subjective errors made by managers in the rating process. The second error I'm concerned about is the similar-to-me error, when appraisers evaluate people against their standards. For appraisals for people with disabilities, I am also concerned that managers might deflate evaluations of people who are different from themselves since they are outside of their frame of reference."

"I can see how the open-ended nature of accommodating employees might pose challenges for over-stretched managers," said Victoria. "Dealing with managers is going to be imperative. How might we think about performance appraisal methods differently from a disability perspective?"

Performance appraisal methods

"Look, we know that 'performance management usually examines individual traits, employee behaviors, or job results' (Belcourt, Singh, Bohlander & Snell, 2014. Pg. 300). It's fine to measure how much employees possess characteristics such as dependability and leadership with the proviso that we might have to rethink what those characteristics mean for disabled employees. For example, we've said that, for some people, punctuality might pose challenges. We can still think of them as dependable if they come to work in the time frame we've negotiated. We might still think of someone as demonstrating leadership, but perhaps that might mean different things for people who have personality disorders. The perennial issue we need to look out for is to ensure that disabled employees are not subjected to prejudice when it comes to the traits for which they are assessed and evaluated."

"Let me see if I understand you correctly," said Victoria. "Ordinarily we might fault an employee who has good ideas when asked for their opinion but otherwise does not offer them. Such a person might be characterized as lacking in self-confidence. You're suggesting we should look at that person's behavior in a different light?"

"Correct. There are many people who have disabilities who lack self-confidence either because perhaps it might be an inherent part of their disorder such as excessive levels of anxiety or perhaps because their disability has left them lacking in self-confidence due to the stigma of their disability. Either way, I think we both agree that there is a moral and business case for not holding it against them when it

106 *Performance management for neurodiversity*

comes to their appraisal. By the way, the same point applies to behavioral methods. We want to make sure that disabled employees are not negatively evaluated for critical incidents that might be disability-related."

"I agree, and I think we can go through the various trait and behavior methods at a later date. What about results methods?"

"I think that this is where there is room for optimism because, as you can see from the literature I have here, current HR thinking supports the idea of a version of management by objectives. Today many organizations, like ours, set up measurable strategic goals using the Balanced Scorecard. 'They then cascade those goals down the organization to reach key performance indicators (KPIs) for each worker that are rationally related to goals at higher levels. KPIs should be few but strategically important' (Belcourt, Singh, Bohlander & Snell, 2014. Pg. 308–309). That this is already accepted thinking bodes well for us because it means we need to adapt it to the particular needs of employees. A second part of the performance management system examines individual behaviors that are tied to competency models for different organizational chart levels or different verticals."

"Our time's almost up," said Victoria. "Any concluding thoughts when it comes to the different types of appraisal interviews?"

"We both know that there are three different kinds of appraisal interviews. One is the *tell and sell interview*, which is all about trying 'to persuade an employee to change in a prescribed manner' (Belcourt, Singh, Bohlander & Snell, 2014. Pg. 311). Another is the *tell and listen interview* that is about trying to communicate someone's 'strong and weak points' (Belcourt, Singh, Bohlander & Snell, 2014. Pg. 311). Finally, *problem-solving interviews* are about 'listening, accepting, and responding to feelings' (Belcourt, Singh, Bohlander & Snell, 2014. Pg. 311).

"Which one is the right type of interview? There is no one correct answer, of course. It depends on the employee's performance. Each might be suitable. I can say the following three things will impact the efficacy of the appraisal interview. First, the pre-existing relationship between the manager and the neurodiverse employee. The better the pre-existing relationship, the more likely it is that the appraisal interview will go smoothly. Second, managers will need to be able to use all these types and to calibrate according to the circumstances. Third, at appraisal interviews, managers should make neurodiversity-related accommodations like providing the text of the appraisal in advance and allowing some neurodiverse employees, when they need them, to use a recording device. Also, managers should not place undue pressure on employees to respond on the spot and allow employees to return for a follow-up interview after a few days."

We invite you now to think about the state of relationships between people with disabilities in your organization and their respective managers. What are trust levels? Do disabled employees feel that their managers are coming through with neurodiversity-related accommodations or not? Do managers trust their employees to open up when they need to do so? If there is a high-trust relationship, then you have a solid foundation on which to build. If disabled employees in your organization do not have a high-trust relationship with their managers, then that should be a red flag, and you know where you will have to roll up your sleeves and get to work. The opposite is also true: if managers do not trust employees, then it will be difficult to secure all the information needed to achieve good job performance from all employees.

How well are the roles of disabled employees in your organization aligned with their strengths? That is a critical question to ask. If you, your disabled employees, and their managers are confident that there is a close correlation between their current roles and their strengths, then this bodes well for all stakeholders. If they battle against their weaknesses, then it is time for all stakeholders to revisit the situation. We feel confident in saying that aligning neurodiverse employees with their strengths will pay dividends for all stakeholders.

Do your managers have the bandwidth to address the neurodiversity-related needs of their employees on an ongoing (and possibly indefinite) basis? If your managers are stretched to their limit, then all the time and resources you put into education and sensitivity training may be futile. Managers stretched to the limit may perceive disabled employees and their seemingly never-ending list of requests as a drain on their time that just won't go away. Since they are already stretched to the limit, they may get frustrated that they just can't seem to get this off their to-do lists. If your disabled employees are assigned to managers who are stretched to the limit, then we suggest that a good step might be to consider assigning them to someone with the bandwidth for their issues.

If your employees who have neurologically based disabilities have good relationships with their managers, if they are in positions aligned with their strengths, and if they are also assigned to managers with the bandwidth to address their neurodiversity-related issues (notwithstanding that they are working in roles aligned with their strengths), then the current state of affairs bodes well for performance management in your organization.

Web-based resources for this chapter

- http://davidguest.com.au/buildingbusinesses/team/performance-management-for-employees-with-a-disability/
- www.hrtips.org/list_1.cfm?c_id=61&view_all=true
- www.eeoc.gov/facts/performance-conduct.html
- www.businessmanagementdaily.com/12371/poor-performance-or-disability-discrimination-keep-good-records-to-prove-youre-not-biased

A tool for reflecting on how to make performance management more sensitive to neurodiverse employees

Directions: Use this tool to guide your thinking, and that of others in your organization, on how to ensure that employees with neurologically based disabilities are not inadvertently penalized during the performance management process. For each question appearing in the left column below, write your answers in the right column. Then compare your thoughts to others in the organization – including the opinions of employees with neurologically based disabilities. While there are no right or wrong answers to the questions, the goal of this tool is to reflect on how the organization's traditional process of performance management can be changed to ensure that employees with neurologically based disabilities are not inadvertently penalized.

	Questions	Your answers
1	How is performance management typically handled in your organization? Describe it step by step.	
2	How should the performance management process be handled in your organization to ensure that employees with neurologically based disabilities are not inadvertently penalized?	
3	What laws, rules, or regulations might affect performance management in your jurisdiction relating to neurodiverse people?	
4	What do workers and managers need to do differently to ensure that employees with neurologically based disabilities are not inadvertently penalized during the performance management process?	

What to do after reading this chapter

1 Broaden your organization's scope of performance recognition to acknowledge attitude and motivation.
2 Identify managers who have the time and bandwidth to pay attention to employees with neurologically based disabilities and their unique needs.
3 Identify managers who do not have the time and bandwidth. What might be done to lighten their load?
4 Take stock of the relationships between any current neurodiverse employees and their managers. Are these relationships currently high trust or low trust?
5 Find out if any teams in your organization have had members from the neurodiverse community in the past. How well was this person integrated into the team? What worked and what did not work?

10 HR trends of the future from a neurodiversity perspective

What trends in HR may affect neurodiverse workers? This chapter offers some predictions.

The trend: digital radically disrupts HR

"Digital technology, including social, gamification, cloud, mobile, big data and consumer applications, is transforming how people carry out their work – and how HR supports them in that effort" (Accenture.com, 2015).

Social applications refer to the advent of software such as Facebook, YouTube, LinkedIn, and others; gamification refers to making learning resemble play through the use of gaming methods; mobile refers to using tablets or smartphones to access communication methods, and big data refers to vast amounts of information about people or events.

The challenge

Some neurodiverse people might face challenges using this technology. That means that HR will need to be more up to date about adaptive technology for people with neurologically based disabilities or need to develop relationships with adaptive technology specialists. They will also need to make sure that vendors are sensitive to the needs of the neurodiverse community and that they can satisfy any existing legal requirements to create websites, games, apps, and so forth so that they are accessible to neurodiverse employees.

The opportunities

Technology is being developed to assist the neurodiverse community.

The trend: reconfiguring the global talent landscape

"HR will transform to adapt to a more global world, including adopting new talent sourcing strategies to match talent with tasks all over the globe, and adopting new

DOI: 10.4324/9781351207478-10

management methods, such as supporting mobile workforces across geographic barriers" (Accenture.com, 2015).

The challenge

Different jurisdictions have very different attitudes and legislation regarding the neurodiverse community. Also, there are very different cultural norms when it comes to people with neurologically based disabilities. For example, in some cultures, openness about disability is more acceptable than in others, where there is still an enormous social stigma attached to having a disability. That might make it even harder to have a coherent organizational culture around the employees with neurologically based disabilities.

The opportunities

Employers who offer forward-thinking approaches to working with the neurodiverse community can have a significant social impact in those jurisdictions by being role models. These companies who offer progressive approaches in less progressive jurisdictions may find themselves at an advantage by being able to tap pools of talent that are out of reach of other less progressive employers in the same jurisdictions.

The trend: tapping skills anywhere, anytime

"Skills gaps are widening, and HR will be increasingly hard-pressed to ensure their organizations have the right talent. HR will need to quickly tap skills when they're needed – and where" (Accenture.com, 2015).

The challenge

Many businesses think in short-term time units – for example, daily worker time reports or quarterly results. In a rush to tap skills quickly when and where they're needed, they might have a bias against making the sort of changes required to draw on the neurodiverse community because those changes take time and are long term.

The opportunity

Those employers willing to make the requisite changes to cater to the neurodiverse community may well find themselves being able to access new pools of talent and thereby alleviate talent shortages because employees with neurologically based disabilities often have higher retention rates than those who do not have disabilities.

The trend: managing your people as a workforce of one

"Customization is poised to revolutionize the way organizations manage their people. They will no longer treat their workforce as a single entity but instead, treat

112 *HR trends of the future from a neurodiversity perspective*

each employee as a 'workforce of one,' offering customized HR and talent management solutions" (Accenture.com, 2015).

The challenge

HR managers will no longer be able to take cookie-cutter approaches. Instead, they will need to wear many more, and different kinds of hats, than they've worn in the past.

The opportunities

If customization is indeed poised to revolutionize the way organizations manage their people, then that bodes well for forward-thinking HR professionals and managers. There may well be faceless pushback when advocating for customized HR and talent management solutions if this is the prevailing trend. Also, those who do face pushback may be better positioned to argue that what they are advocating for is increasingly the norm and not the exception since this is the way the world is changing in any case. The trends relate to the notion of *mass customization*, which means finding cost-effective ways to offer products or services on a large scale but give individuals the ability to modify those products or services to meet their unique needs.

The trend: the rise of the extended workforce

"Organizations will leverage the new extended workforce-A global network of outside contractors, outsourcing partners, vendors, and other nontraditional employees. HR will redefine its mission and mandate to maximize the extended workforce's strategic value" (Accenture.com, 2015).

The challenge

How to ensure that this extended workforce is disability friendly and meets the needs of an employer's disabled employees.

The opportunities

The flip side of the challenge is that HR could potentially draw on a vastly greater network of contractors, partners, and vendors to provide a broader array of supportive products, knowledge, and skills than those that are available locally.

The trend: shattering the boundaries of HR

"HR will evolve from being a defined, stand-alone function that administers HR and talent management processes to one that spans disciplines and crosses boundaries to deliver cross-functional, holistic employee experiences" (Accenture.com, 2015).

The challenge

HR professionals will need to step out of their comfort zone and support their disabled employees in ways that they have not done so before.

The opportunities

The greater the depth and breadth of HR's reach into an organization, the more hope there is that it will succeed in creating sustainable organization-wide change. This trend should give rise to optimism that revising the entire end-to-end talent management process, from a disability perspective, will be an enduring change rather than a management flavor of the month.

The trend: talent management meets the science of human behavior

"As new insights into brain science and human behavior emerge – and as analytics finally enable organizations to test hypotheses and form conclusions by analyzing a newly available treasure trove of data – HR will arm itself with the tools and insights of a scientist to drive better performance from their workforces" (Accenture.com, 2015).

The challenge

HR may be challenged on storing, managing, and accessing private data. They will need to determine if existing privacy policies and procedures are adequate to handle this. How will managers and HR professionals work with this kind of information that has heretofore been outside the scope of their professional practice?

The opportunities

HR professionals could become more aware of, and sensitive to, the unique issues, needs, and challenges of the neurodiverse community, as well as their talents and what they have to offer. That could lead to HR being better prepared to align employees more efficiently in ways that are beneficial to the employee and the organization. A significant paradigm shift might flow from this trend, namely that employers will increasingly come to view people from the neurodiverse population as possessing valuable talents rather than as problem employees.

The trend: HR drives the agile organization

"As the world becomes increasingly unpredictable, organizations that can adapt to changing business conditions will outperform the competition. HR will reshape itself so that it becomes the critical driver of agility" (Accenture.com, 2015).

The challenge

The essential point is that businesses striving for agility expect their workforce to become more responsive and nimble. If HR is to become the critical driver of agility, then it will need to be aware of the following two challenges. First, that employers do not dismiss the neurodiverse community as a result of stereotypical thinking that they are slow, unresponsive, and need more hand-holding and, second, that agility is developed in a way that employees with neurologically based disabilities are not left behind. Workers and managers may need to be made aware of ways to ensure that, with reasonable accommodations, neurodiverse employees may be as productive as those who are neurotypical.

The opportunity

Many people from within the neurodiverse population have a propensity for skills that can be used to enhance an organization's competitiveness. For example, people with autism are sometimes exceptionally gifted with specific skills – savants are a familiar archetype, as the movie *Rain Man* has shown – and some people with OCD have been found to excel at detailed work.

The trend: HR must navigate risk and privacy in a more complex world

"HR will adopt risk management strategies covering everything from protecting confidential information and data, to risks associated with weak hiring or turnover of talent" (Accenture.com, 2015).

The challenge

Risk management strategies could be a problem if increased focus on risk mitigation leads HR to try to avoid hiring people with neurologically based disabilities because they are perceived to be too much of a risk.

The opportunities

This trend could be good news if this means that HR will be better prepared to manage the sensitive and confidential information of neurodiverse employees.

The trend: social media drives the democratization of work

"Instead of relying on solutions dictated from the top of the organization, organizations will be populated with knowledge workers who harness social media to create solutions in conjunction with each other, thereby radically disrupting organizational structures, hierarchy, and job titles" (Accenture.com, 2015).

The challenge

Neurodiverse employees may not be as savvy with social media as their colleagues. Collaboration, whether it be online or in person, will be central to this trend. To a certain extent, persons with disabilities depend on organizational structures, hierarchy, and job titles to know where to go to receive the accommodations they need and to navigate their way through organizational complexity. Disrupted structures, hierarchies, and job titles might make it might more complicated to figure out who to turn to and where responsibilities lie. Finally, collaboration is central to this trend that could disadvantage those with weaker emotional intelligence and social intelligence skills. This potential pitfall is of particular importance because (as mentioned in an earlier chapter), often, people with various disabilities struggle to master social intelligence skills. They may also exhibit behaviors that lead others to label them incorrectly as lacking in emotional intelligence and social skills.

The opportunities

This trend might also present opportunities for self-actualization in the workplace. Since neurodiverse employees often do not fit neatly into clearly defined roles, some of them may do well in varied roles that play to their extreme strengths and avoid their weaknesses. The world where conventional structures, hierarchy, and job titles have been disrupted may bode well for neurodiverse employees, who would not thrive in straitjacketed roles, by making it more conducive for them to find the modified roles to which they might be better suited.

As organizations strive to become more agile, they will transform processes.

A parting word

As the world's population ages, employers will be forced to cultivate employees from groups that have been traditionally overlooked. One such group are people who experience various neurologically based disabilities. We have referred to them as the neurodiverse community. This chapter concludes the book by pointing the way toward the future.

But the future belongs to you. You must now:

- Make others aware of the need to make workplace conditions more welcoming to all employees.
- Teach and train people what they should do to be more welcoming to all employees – including those who experience neurologically based disabilities.
- Take active steps to make Human Resources Management more supportive of the needs of workers, including those from the neurodiverse community.

If you follow the path outlined in this book, we feel confident that you will greatly increase your prospects of Winning the Talent War through Neurodivergence by creating workplaces where people with neurologically based disabilities can thrive.

Bibliography

Accenture.com, 2015. *The Future of HR: A Radically Different Proposition*. Available at www.accenture.com/t20150523T024235__w__/be-en/_acnmedia/Accenture/Convers ion-Assets/DotCom/Documents/Global/PDF/Dualpub_14/Accenture-Future-of-HR-Overview.pdf. Accessed on 12/14/2017.

American Academy of Neurology, n.d. *Compelling Statistics*. Available at www.aan.com/uploadedFiles/Website_Library_Assets/Documents/6.Public_Policy/1.Stay_Informed/4.Public_Policy_Resources/compell.pdf. Accessed on 12/05/2017.

American Psychiatric Association. (2013). *Diagnostic and Statistical Manual of Mental Disorders* (fifth ed.). Washington, DC: Author.

Asperger's Society of Ontario, n.d. *Common Traits*. Available at www.aspergers.ca/what-is-asperger-syndrome/common-traits/. Accessed on 01/21/2018.

Autism Canada, 2017. *We Are All Unique*. Available at https://autismcanada.org/about-aut ism/characteristics/. Accessed on 01/21/2018.

Bauer, T., 2010. *Onboarding Employees: Maximizing Success*. Alexandria, VA: The Society for Human Resources Management (SHRM).

Belcourt, M., Singh, P., Bohlander, G., & Snell, S. 2014. *Managing Human Resources*. Toronto, ON: Nelson Education Ltd.

Brainfacts.org, n.d. *Neurological Diseases and Disorders A-Z from NINDS*. Available at www.brainfacts.org/diseases-and-disorders/neurological-disorders-az. Accessed on 12/05/2017.

BrainyQuote.com, n.d. Available at www.brainyquote.com/quotes/quotes/p/peterdruck131 069.html. Accessed on 12/12/2017.

Centers for Disease Control and Prevention, 2016. *Prevalence and Characteristics of Autism Spectrum Disorder among Children Aged 8 Years: Autism and Developmental Disabilities Monitoring Network, 11 Sites, United States, 2012*. Available at www.cdc.gov/mmwr/volumes/65/ss/ss6503a1.htm. Accessed on 12/05/2017.

Cnn.com, 2017. *American Generation Fast Facts*. Available at www.cnn.com/2013/11/06/us/baby-boomer-generation-fast-facts. Accessed on 12/14/2017.

Cornell Chronicle, 2013. *Report Finds It Pays to Hire Disabled Workers*. Available at http://news.cornell.edu/stories/2013/03/report-finds-it-pays-hire-disabled-workers. Accessed on 12/02/2017.

CureResearch.com, 2005. *Basic Summary for Learning Disabilities*. Available at www.curer esearch.com/l/learning_disabilities/basics_printer.htm. Accessed on 12/05/2017.

Davis, R.D., 1992. *Test for Dyslexia: 37 Common Traits*. Available at www.dyslexia.com/library/symptoms.htm. Accessed on 01/21/2018.

Bibliography 117

Felicetti, K., n.d. *These Major Tech Companies Are Making Autism Hiring a Priority.* Available at www.monster.com/technology/a/autism-hiring-initiatives-tech. Accessed on 12/05/2017.

Globe and Mail, 2015. *Boom, Bust and Economic Headaches.* Available at www.theglobe andmail.com/globe-investor/retirement/the-boomer-shift-how-canadas-economy-is-hea ded-for-majorchange/article27159892/. Accessed on 12/05/2017.

Globe and Mail, 2017. *Google's Secret: Hire People for What They Don't Know Yet.* Available at www.theglobeandmail.com/report-on-business/careers/management/goog les-secret-hire-people-for-what-they-dont-know-yet/article21749724/. Accessed on 12/05/2017.

Hallowell, E., 2005. *Overloaded Circuits: Why Smart People Underperform.* Available at https://hbr.org/2005/01/overloaded-circuits-why-smart-people-underperform. Accessed on 12/03/2017.

HelpGuide.org, n.d. *Obsessive-Compulsive Disorder (OCD).* Available at www.helpguide. org/articles/anxiety/obssessive-compulsive-disorder-ocd.htm#signs. Accessed on 01/21/2018.

India Times, 2015. *India, China Face Prospect of Substantial Population Aging.* Available at http://articles.economictimes.indiatimes.com/2015-08-12/news/65490478_1_populat ion-growth-population-division-older-population. Accessed on 12/05/2017.

The Innovative Educator, 2011. Available at http://theinnovativeeducator.blogspot.com/2011/09/25-incredible-assistive-technologies.html. Accessed on 12/07/2017.

Learning Disabilities Association of Canada, 2015a. *Official Definition of Learning Disabilities.* Available at www.ldac-acta.ca/learn-more/ld-defined. Accessed on 12/14/2017.

Learning Disabilities Association of Canada, 2015b. *A Working Description of Learning Disabilities.* Available at www.ldac-acta.ca/learn-more/ld-defined/a-working-descript ion-of-learning-disabilities. Accessed on 12/14/2017.

LoGiudice, K., 2008. *Common Characteristics of Adult Dyslexia.* Available at www.dysle xia.com/library/adult-symptoms.htm. Accessed on 01/21/2018.

Manzella Report, n.d. *The Real Cause and Impact of China's Labor Shortage.* Available at www.manzellareport.com/index.php/special/the-real-cause-and-impact-of-china-s-labor-shortage. Accessed on 12/05/2017.

Medscape, 2006. *Mental Illness and Employment Discrimination.* Available at www.medsc ape.com/viewarticle/542517_2. Accessed on 12/05/2017.

National Institute of Mental Health, 2015. *Any Mental Illness (AMI) among U.S. Adults.* Available at www.nimh.nih.gov/health/statistics/prevalence/any-mental-illness-ami-among-us-adults.shtml. Accessed on 12/05/2017.

Ontario Ministry of Community and Social Services, 2010. *Myths and Facts.* Available at www.mcss.gov.on.ca/documents/en/talent/employer/information/tips/mythsAndFa cts_en1.pdf. Accessed on 12/05/2017.

Randstad, 2016. *Build Your Employer Brand: A Strategic Approach to Recruitment and Retention.* Available at www.randstad.ca/workforce360-trends/archives/a-strategic-appro ach-to-recruitment-and-retention_347. Accessed on 12/10/2017.

Randstad, 2017. *Develop an Employer Brand That Employees Love in 5 Steps.* Available at www.randstad.ca/workforce360-trends/archives/5-steps-to-build-up-your-employer-brand_621/. Accessed on 12/10/2017.

Rothwell, W., Graber, J. & McCormick, N., 2012. *Lean But Agile: Rethink Workforce Planning and Gain a True Competitive Advantage.* New York: AMACOM.

118   *Bibliography*

Rothwell, W., Sterns, H., Spokus, D. & Reaser, J., 2008. *Working Longer: New Strategies for Managing, Training, and Retaining Older Employees*. New York: AMACOM.

Rothwell, W. et al., 2013. *Performance Consulting: Applying Performance Improvement in Human Resource Development*. San Francisco: Pfeiffer.

Science Daily, 2013. *Learning Disabilities Affect Up to Ten Percent of Children*. Available at www.sciencedaily.com/releases/2013/04/130418142309.htm. Accessed on 12/05/2017.

Shamir, L., 2012. *Recruiters: Your Days Are Numbered*. Available at www.eremedia.com/ere/recruiters-your-days-are-numbered/. Accessed on 12/10/2017.

Social Thinking, n.d. Available at www.socialthinking.com/what-is-social-thinking. Accessed on 12/12/2017.

Speech-Language and Audiology Canada, June 2017. Available at www.sac-oac.ca/news-events/events/13th-international-conference-neurology-and-neurosurgery. Accessed on 01/15/2018.

Stuart, H., 2006. *Mental Illness and Employment Discrimination*. Available at www.medscape.com/viewarticle/542517_2. Accessed on 12/14/2017.

University at Buffalo, Graduate School of Education Online, n.d. *Rehabilitation Counseling MS*. Available at www.buffalo.edu/gse/online/programs/masters/rehab.html. Accessed on 12/07/2017.

Un.org, 2002. *World Population Ageing: 1950–2050*. Available at www.un.org/esa/population/publications/worldageing19502050/. Accessed on 12/05/2017.

Vietnam Briefing, 2014. *Foreign Companies Report Labor and Skills Shortage in Vietnam*. Available at www.vietnam-briefing.com/news/foreign-companies-report-labor-skills-shortage-vietnam.html/. Accessed on 12/05/2017.

VRA Canada, 2017. *VRA and CVRP*. Available at www.vracanada.com/about-us/vra-and-cvrp/. Accessed on 12/08/2017.

Washington Post, 2014. *Do 10,000 Baby Boomers Retire Every Day?* Available at www.washingtonpost.com/news/fact-checker/wp/2014/07/24/do-10000-baby-boomers-retire-every-day/. Accessed on 12/05/2017.

Webmd.com, n.d. *10 Problems That Could Mean Adult ADHD*. Available at www.webmd.com/add-adhd/guide/10-symptoms-adult-adhd?page=2. Accessed on 01/21/2018.

World Health Organization, 2017. *Depression Fact Sheet*. Available at www.who.int/mediacentre/factsheets/fs369/en/. Accessed on 12/05/2017.

Zolfagharifard, E., 2014. *First Impressions Really DO Count: Employers Make Decisions about Job Applicants in under Seven Minutes*. Available at www.dailymail.co.uk/sciencetech/article-2661474/First-impressions-really-DO-count-Employers-make-decisions-job-applicants-seven-minutes.html#ixzz434hsscJ3. Accessed on 12/15/2017.

Index

accountability 31
administrative assistant job
   description 22–25
Americans with Disabilities Act 5
autism 4
autism spectrum disorder 4

Baby Boomers 2, 3–4
Bauer, T. 73
Belcourt, M. 19, 27, 30, 50, 100
Bohlander, G. 19, 27, 30, 50, 100

career development initiatives 55–58
career management 50–51; blending
   goals of the individual employees
   with goals of the organization 52–53;
   career development initiatives 55–58;
   identifying career opportunities and
   requirements 53–55; matching individual
   and organizational needs 51–58;
   tool for reflecting on 59
classroom instruction 93
competency-based analysis 17
compressed work week 33–34
critical incident method (CIM) 15–16
cross-training 95
CureResearch.com 4

democratization of work 114–115
demographic issues 2–4, 110–111
*Diagnostic and Statistical Manual of
   Mental Disorders (DSM), The* 4
digital technology 110
disability perspective in strong employment
   brand 41–44
Drucker, P. 82
dyslexia 4

employee empowerment 29–31
employee involvement groups (EIs) 31–33

employee selection 11, 61–62;
   determining validity of tests used
   for 67–68; employment equity and
   65–66; employment interviews for
   62–65; pre-employment tests for 66–67;
   reaching a decision in 68–69; tool for
   reflecting on 70
employment equity 65–66
empowerment, employee 29–31
equity, employment 65–66
evaluation, training program 94–95
external recruiting channels 44–47

feedback 98–99; tools for 80–83
flexible work schedules 33–36
flextime 34
four C stages of onboarding 74

global talent landscape 2–4, 110–111
groups 31–33

human resources management (HRM):
   challenge in 1–2; digital disruptions of
   110; driving the agile organization
   113–114; global demographic issues
   in 2–4, 110–111; job analysis in 9;
   managing people as workforce of one
   111–112; navigating risk and privacy in
   a more complex world 114; parting word
   on 115; redefined for neurodiversity 6,
   7; rise of extended workforce and 112;
   shattering the boundaries of 112–113;
   social media driving democratization of
   work and 114–115; talent management
   meeting science of human behavior
   and 113; tapping skills anywhere,
   anytime 111

individual and organization needs, career
   management for 51–58

120 *Index*

internships 92–93
interviews, employment 62–65

job analysis: as collaborative effort 13–14;
   competency-based analysis 17; critical
   incident method (CIM) 15–16; position
   analysis questionnaire (PAQ) system
   15; strategic HR planning and 9–10;
   task inventory analysis 16; tool for
   reflecting on 37
job characteristics 29
job descriptions: biases and 11; problems
   with 18–20; reinvented for the
   neurodiverse 17–20; tool for reflecting
   on 37; welcome-sign 22–25; writing
   clear and specific 20
job design 25–33; behavioral concerns and
   27; employee empowerment and
   29–31; flexible work schedules 33–36;
   for groups 31–33; job characteristics and
   29; job enrichment and 27–29
job duties or essential functions 18
job enrichment 27–29
job identification section 18
job requirements 9; fictional frame on 10;
   legal compliance in 13; performance
   appraisal and 12–13; recruitment and
   10–11; training and development and 12;
   understanding biases in 11
job specification section 18
job titles 17
job-sharing 34–35

labor demand 3
learning: principles of 90–91; readiness and
   motivation for 90
legal compliance 13

National Institute of Neurological
   Conditions and Stroke 4
needs assessment 86–89
neurodiversity: career management for
   (*see* career management); definition
   of 4; employee selection for (*see*
   employee selection); facts and figures
   about 4–5; flexible work schedules
   for 33–36; job descriptions reinvented
   for (*see* job descriptions); job design
   for 25–33; neurodiverse community
   1, 4; onboarding for (*see* onboarding);
   performance management for (*see*
   performance management); recruiting
   for (*see* recruiting); redefining Human

Resources Management for 5–6; in teams
   31–33; training and development for
   (*see* training and development)
new employee adjustment 74–78

occupational therapists 26
on-the-job training (OJT) 91–92
Onboarding Employees: Maximizing
   Success 73
onboarding for neurodiversity 72–74;
   coaching and support for 80; feedback
   tools for 80–83; four C's of 74; short-
   term outcomes of 74–78; support
   tools and processes for 79–80; tool
   for reflecting on 84; what happens
   during 78–79
online instruction 94
organization analysis 87–88
organizational/corporate culture 30, 90, 101

performance management 98–99;
   developing effect appraisal programs for
   100–101; failure of appraisals programs
   and 99–100; neurodiversity concerns
   and 100; performance appraisal methods
   for 12–13, 105–107; strategic relevance
   and 101–104; tool for reflecting on 108;
   training appraisers and 104–105
person analysis 88–89
position analysis questionnaire (PAS)
   system 15
pre-employment tests 66–67; validity
   of 67–68
problem-solving interviews 106

Randstad Canada 41
Realistic Job Previews (RJPs) 78
recruiting 10–11, 38–39; building a strong
   employment brand from disability
   perspective and 41–44; critical
   attributes for recruiters and 39–41;
   external channels for 44–47; tool for
   reflecting on 48
return on investment (ROI) of
   training 94–95

short-term outcomes of onboarding 74–78
Singh, P. 19, 27, 30, 50, 100
Snell, S. 19, 27, 30, 50, 100
social media 114–115
Social Thinking 63
strategic relevance 101–104
strong employment brand 41–44

Index 121

task analysis 88
task inventory analysis 16
teams 31–33; training and
    cross-training of 95
telecommuting 35–36
tell and sell interview 106
training and development 12, 86;
    classroom instruction 93; internships
    92–93; learner readiness and motivation
    for 90; methods for non-managerial
    employees 91–92; objectives of 89;
    online instruction 94; phase four:
    evaluating the training program
94–95; phase one: conducting the
needs assessment 86–89; phase three:
implementing the training program
91–94; phase two: designing the training
program 89–91; principles of learning
and 90–91; scope of 86; team 95; tool for
reflecting on 96; training appraisers and
104–105

vocational rehabilitation 26

welcome-sign job descriptions 22–25
Winner, M. G. 63